SOUTH ASIAN
POLITICAL SYSTEMS

General Editor
RICHARD L. PARK

*The Politics of Nepal: Persistence
and Change in an Asian Monarchy*
by Leo E. Rose *and* Margaret W. Fisher

*The Politics of Pakistan:
A Constitutional Quest*
by Richard S. Wheeler

The Politics of Afghanistan
by Richard S. Newell

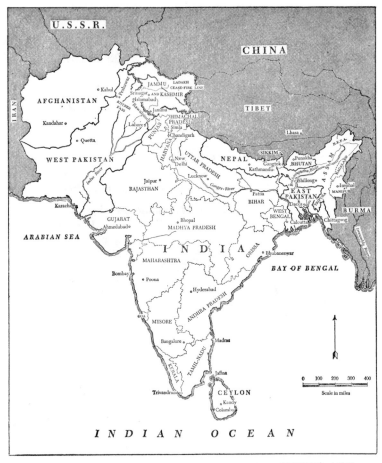

U.S.S.R.

CHINA

IRAN

AFGHANISTAN

Kabul

Peshawar

Kandahar

KHYBER PASS

Quetta

WEST PAKISTAN

Karachi

Indus River

JAMMU

LADAKH
CEASE-FIRE LINE

Srinagar
Islamabad

AND KASHMIR

Rawalpindi

Jammu

Lahore

HIMACHAL
PRADESH

Simla

Chandigarh

PUNJAB

HARYANA

New
Delhi

UTTAR PRADESH

Jaipur

RAJASTHAN

Lucknow

Ganges River

TIBET

NEPAL

Lhasa

Kathmandu

SIKKIM

Gangtok

Punakha

BHUTAN

Patna

BIHAR

Shillong

Brahmaputra River

N.E.F.A.

ASSAM

NAGALAND

Imphal

MANIPUR

ARABIAN SEA

GUJARAT

Ahmedabad

Bhopal

MADHYA PRADESH

I N D I A

EAST
PAKISTAN

Dacca

WEST
BENGAL

Calcutta

Chittagong

BURMA

Irrawaddy River

MAHARASHTRA

Bombay

Poona

Hyderabad

ORISSA

Bhubaneswar

BAY OF BENGAL

GOA

MYSORE

ANDHRA PRADESH

Bangalore

Madras

KERALA

TAMIL NADU

Jaffna

Trivandrum

CEYLON

Kandy

Colombo

0   100   200   300   400

Scale in miles

N

I N D I A N   O C E A N

SOUTH ASIA

The Politics of Afghanistan

RICHARD S. NEWELL

Cornell University Press

ITHACA AND LONDON

099530

*First published 1972 by Cornell University Press.
Published in the United Kingdom by
Cornell University Press Ltd.,
2–4 Brook Street, London W1Y 1AA.*

International Standard Book Number 0-8014-0688-9
Library of Congress Catalog Card Number 78-176487

PRINTED IN THE UNITED STATES OF AMERICA
BY VAIL-BALLOU PRESS, INC.

*Librarians: Library of Congress cataloging information
appears on the last page of the book.*

To Noël, Victoria, and Doré

Foreword

Serious study of modern South Asia is a relatively recent development in the United States. It began shortly after World War II, and was made possible by opportunities for language study and research in the region. Scholarly work on current South Asian themes, however, rests upon older academic traditions that emphasized principally the philosophy, religion, and classical literature of these ancient civilizations. This series, "South Asian Political Systems," is addressed to contemporary political problems, but is presented in the context of institutions and value systems that were centuries in the making.

Over the past quarter century, humanists and social scientists in Asia, Europe, the United States, and elsewhere throughout the world have worked together to study modern South Asian cultures. Their efforts have been encouraged by a recognition of the importance of the rapid rise of nationalism in Asia in the twentieth century, by the decline, hastened by the war, of Western imperial systems, and by the appearance of dozens of independent states since the founding of the United Nations. Scholars were made increasingly aware that the South Asian peoples were not anonymous masses or abstract representatives of distant traditions. They were, like us, concerned with their own political affairs, with raising families, building houses, constructing industries, educating the young, and creating better societies. They were nourished by their heritage, but they also struggled to devise political institutions, economic processes, and social organizations that were responsive to modern needs. And their needs were, and continue to be, great.

It was an awareness of these realities that encouraged private foundations and agencies of government to sponsor intensive field work in South Asia, including firsthand observation of day-to-day life and opportunities to discover and use rare source material. India has received the most attention, in part because of its size and intrinsic importance, in part because scholars have concentrated on teaching Indian languages, and research tends to be done where the languages are understood. More and more the other countries of South Asia—Pakistan, Nepal, Ceylon, and Afghanistan—have begun to attract scholarly attention. Whereas in the late 1940's one was hard pressed to find literature about the region, except in journalistic accounts or in British imperial histories, in the 1970's competent monographs and reliable periodicals are abundantly available. Today one can draw from an impressive bibliography on South Asia, including a commendable list of political works.

It remains true, however, that recent South Asian studies have been largely monographic—books that examine narrow themes in detail and that appeal to a small group of specialists who happen to be concerned with these themes. There are few broad guides to the politics of the countries of South Asia. This series has been designed to fill part of the need.

One of the problems in writing introductory works is

that learning about a foreign culture is never a simple process. Experience tells us that each political system is imbedded in a broader social system, which in turn has roots in a particular history and a unique set of values. Language transmits culture, so one way to approach an unfamiliar culture is through the close study of language and literature. Knowledge of history, or of the arts, or of social organization offers another path to understanding.

The focus of this series is on political systems. Each author starts with a common organizational framework—brief history, political dynamics, political structure, continuing problems—and weaves in unique factors. For India, a complex federal organization of government and a varied and changing political party system require emphasis. For Pakistan, the constitutional dilemma is the most crucial issue. For Nepal and Afghanistan, monarchical traditions in conflict with pressures to modernize necessitate treatments that are more historically oriented. Ceylon, too, has political problems, especially ethnic and religious, not readily comparable with others. Used together the books should provide excellent opportunities for comparison and contrast.

Professor Richard S. Newell lived and traveled in Afghanistan in the mid-1960's and has been particularly concerned with Afghan political affairs since the adoption of the 1964 Constitution. His book offers an introduction to the political development of a society which has been neglected by social scientists. By stressing the theme of change within continuity the author has been able to demonstrate the uniqueness and significance of Afghanistan's efforts to come to terms with modernization.

RICHARD L. PARK

Ann Arbor, Michigan

Preface

Few peoples possess a past or a culture as suited to romantic treatment as do the Afghans. Their tenacious hold on a barren landscape, their dignity, their hospitality, their esteem for valor and piety, the mystique lent them by remoteness, uniqueness, and commitment to tradition offer an inexhaustible supply of material to excited writers. Also contributing to this romanticism has been the Afghan struggle to remold their government to meet the needs of the twentieth century. Their monarchy, whose authority was until recently based upon unstable tribal loyalties, must now satisfy growing demands for popular participation and modern services.

Afghanistan has not been alone in facing such challenges, but there have been special elements in the kingdom's experience. Its royal government is one of the few to survive outside of Europe; no other Islamic people has been as successful in fending off European political control. This relative freedom did not exempt Afghans from pressures for change induced from outside. Their leaders have been caught increasingly between the need for innovation and the restraints imposed by tradition. And in attempting to steer a course which combines change and continuity the Afghans have won the assistance of a remarkably wide assortment of foreign benefactors. At times such generosity has threatened to overwhelm the kingdom's subsistence economy with dams, roads, and factories, rubles, pounds, marks, and dollars.

Great as the temptation toward romanticism may be in writing about Afghanistan, the rewards of sober analysis are even greater. This study aims to introduce the concepts and information necessary to a general understanding of the political forces at play in Afghanistan. It focuses upon the setting and the processes of contemporary political change and emphasizes ideas, institutions, policies, and goals. The first two chapters provide a description of the physical, sociocultural, and historical factors which shaped premodern Afghan life. Then follows an analysis of the contemporary structure and functions of government, and a chapter devoted to recent economic changes and the role of foreign assistance. The concluding discussion concentrates upon the current Afghan attempts to make parliamentary democracy workable despite the threats of political instability and economic crisis.

Relatively little attention is paid the personal, familial, or tribal dynamics behind contemporary events, primarily because of the lack of reliable evidence. Reports of factions, rivalries, enmities, alliances, and ambitions are plentiful in Afghanistan, but definitive information is scarce. Even when genuine, evidence based upon personal factors tends to distort or obscure the causes of events. Caution must be applied especially to the most recent political developments. Thus, little specific reference is made to the emergence of charismatic leaders, a phenomenon which began shortly after the adoption of the 1964 Constitution. Appraisal of this trend awaits study by Afghans themselves. Few outsiders are in a position to

explicate the personal dimensions of Afghan political behavior.

This book is largely the product of the accomplishments
and generosity of others. I am indebted to Vartan Gregorian of the University of Texas, Leon Poullada of
Princeton University, and Ibrahim Pourhadi of the Library of Congress for instructive comments, materials, and
encouragement. Louis Jacob of the Asian Reference Department of the University of Pennsylvania library made
a summer's work at his library productive and pleasant.
Jamila Seraj of the Asia Foundation's Kabul office, Howard Nyberg of the Vector Corporation of Chicago, and
Robert Flaten, Afghanistan Desk Officer of the United
States Department of State, furnished information unavail-
able elsewhere. Baqui Yousufzai of the University of In-
diana read the manuscript at a critical stage and is responsible for several material improvements. Muhammad
S. Daneshjo of the Afghanistan Embassy in Washington
provided briefings on the most recent events and supplied
the latest editions of the Kabul *Times*.

I am especially grateful to Daisy and Arthur Paul of
Philadelphia for their hospitality, which allowed me to use
Arthur's unique collection on contemporary Afghanistan.
Arthur Paul, William McCulloch, and John Perry are
responsible for teaching me most of what I have learned
about economic development in the kingdom.

The following support also turned out to be essential:
a Summer Research Award (1970) from the University of
Northern Iowa, the meticulous corrections made by Jane
and Michael Weininger, the generosity of Lyn and Mike
Edwards, the transcript of a long summer's dictation by

Maxine Schwartz, and the clerical favors rendered by Eleanor Eiklor. I am grateful to John Kirby of Northern Iowa for assistance with the map of Afghanistan.

Above all I owe thanks to Richard Park, general editor of this series, who provided the opportunity to write this book and then gave the gentle but firm guidance needed to bring it to completion.

RICHARD S. NEWELL

Cedar Falls, Iowa

Contents

Maps

Tables

The Politics of
Afghanistan

1. Physical and
Social Setting

Afghan society has been molded by an extraordinary set of physical and environmental factors. It inherited an austere climate and a forbidding terrain. It has held a crossroads location permitting close contact with the civilizations of China, India, and the Middle East. These influences stamped traits upon Afghan life which have emphasized survival and a strong sense of independence within an over-all pattern of ethnic and cultural diversity. Physical resources offer the country at least modest opportunities for industrial and other forms of modern development. Nevertheless, environmental factors have hampered Afghan attempts to build a strong, modern political system.

The Land

Afghanistan's boundaries surround the massive Hindu Kush Range which extends southwestward across the country like a great gnarled hand. The Hindu Kush is a western offshoot of the Himalayas. In its far northeast, peaks frequently reach higher than 20,000 feet. Far more than half of the country's land surface is covered by this range and its subdivisions.

Most of the Hindu Kush is a desolate wilderness of bare

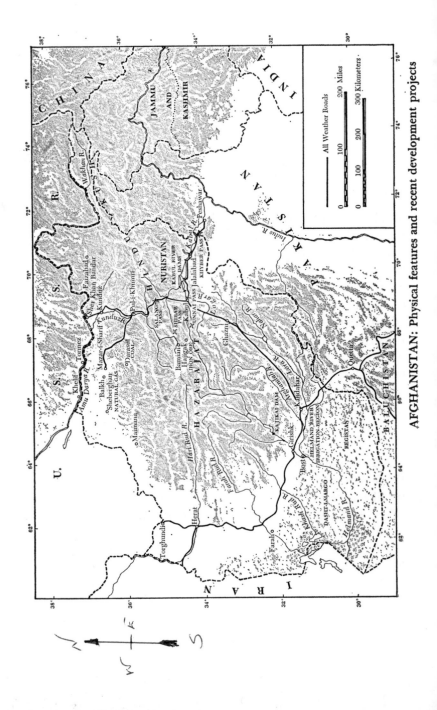

AFGHANISTAN: Physical features and recent development projects

mountains, deep valleys, barren rock, and little soil. Occasionally there are fertile valleys where soil and water come together. These include the valley of Bamian, nearly in the center of the Hindu Kush, and the Kabul, Logar, and Koh-i-Stan valleys on its eastern side. Farther out from the core of the mountains the elevation drops away. Hills give way to plateaus, especially in the northern, western, and southern borderlands. Onto these plateaus flow the several major rivers which rise from the snows of the central mountains.

Where these rivers have intersected major trade routes, several persistent city sites have developed. The combination of adequate soil and water brought down from the hills, and economic as well as cultural stimulation made possible the ancient towns of Herat, Balkh, Kandahar, Ghazni, and Kabul.

In the north the Kunduz River has watered the plain of Bactria and over its long history of settlement this valley has supported several cities. Kunduz is its largest contemporary center. To its west lie the modern towns of Mazar-i-Sharif and Balkh, a trading mart long before the Christian era. Herat faces the Iranian border in the west. It dominates the large, fertile valley of the Hari Rud, Afghanistan's largest westward-flowing river. Kandahar is the largest city in the south. It too has an extensive irrigable plain created by the Arghandab and other tributaries of the Helmand River.

Kabul is not a city of the plateau, but it has prospered because its hinterland contains a system of fertile valleys at elevations above 5,000 feet.

Afghanistan's border regions are generally desolate and dry. South of Kandahar lies the wilderness of Registan, a desert which can only support nomads and their herds. Similar desolation prevails in the Dasht-i-Margo of the southwest. Along the western frontier with Iran the land is almost as dry, and the far northern frontier marked by the Amu Darya is likewise nearly desert. Even among the valleys of the Sulaiman Range, which runs roughly parallel to the eastern border, there are extensive areas of unpopulated wilderness. Rugged at its center and relatively flat at its peripheries, the Afghan landscape has induced the bulk of the sedentary population to concentrate at those few hospitable connecting points where the waters of the mountains meet the plateaus.

Climate

The nearly continuous motion of continental fronts southeastward through Russian Central Asia dominates Afghanistan's climate. Its most prominent features are aridity and sharp seasonal contrasts. For most of the country rainfall is restricted to March, April, and May. During the winter and early spring, snow collects at elevations above 2,000 feet. Most crops depend upon the permanent snowfields in the central parts of the Hindu Kush and upon techniques for catching and storing the runoff. Few sections of Afghanistan average more than ten inches of rain per year.

In the desert regions temperatures rise to extremely high levels in the summer, reaching over 120° F. in the south. The far northern plain experiences temperatures of 106° to 110° F. Even at nearly 6,000 feet the clear air of Kabul allows enough solar radiation to push temperatures above 100°. The winters are nearly as extreme. Temperatures drop below freezing in the desert regions and frequently below 0° F. at Kabul. Spring in the moderate elevations tends to be cool and wet; fall is warmer, but dry and dusty. These sharp variations of heat together with the general dryness severely limit Afghan agriculture and dramatize the economic, cultural, and even psychological significance of the major rivers.

Agricultural Resources

Topography and climate determine that most of the productive land in Afghanistan is concentrated in a few valleys or straddles river beds in the plateaus. No comprehensive survey of land use has been completed, but estimates of cultivable land range between 6 to 18 million acres or from about 4 to 12 per cent of the land surface. The most recent survey indicates that more than 8 million acres (3.4 million hectares) are currently under the plow (see Table 1). Most of this land is located at or near those major centers of population where the rivers widen out onto the plains. In addition to Bactria, Herat, Kandahar, and Kabul, this includes Jalalabad near the Khyber Pass and Farah in the southwest and the Helmand basin below Girishk. Most of the cultivated soil is watered by irrigation systems which use rivers, canals, wells, or tunnels. While the cultivated area can be enlarged by modern land reclamation and irrigation techniques, Afghanistan has neither the soil nor the water resources to support population densities which approach those of nearby India or Pakistan.

Widespread erosion produced by deforestation and sheep grazing has also limited Afghan agriculture. Extensive forests are found only in the valleys along the eastern border and on some of the higher upland ridges in the

Table 1. Agriculture in Afghanistan: Land utilization and production, 1967–1968

Major crops	Production in tons	Yield per hectare in tons
Wheat	2,354,000	1.1
Corn	773,000	1.7
Barley	361,000	1.1
Rice	402,000	2.0
Cotton	71,000	1.3
Sugar beets	62,000	13.7
Sugar cane	57,000	23.7
Oilseeds	36,000	0.9
Vegetables	654,000	7.2
Fruit	834,000	6.1
Others	39,000	

Total area available for cultivation: 7,844,000 hectares

Total irrigated area: 5,340,000 hectares

Total area under crops: 3,406,000 hectares *

Source: Royal Government of Afghanistan, Ministry of Planning, Department of Statistics, *Survey of Progress, 1968–69* (Kabul, 1969), pp. S-20, 21.

* Most of the 4,438,000 hectare difference between land available for cultivation and land under crops can be assumed to be lying fallow although much fallow land is used for pasturage. One hectare equals 2.46 acres.

central Hindu Kush. With an area of nearly 250,000 square miles, the kingdom has no more than 1.5 million acres of timber.

Until recently Afghanistan was usually self-sufficient in its major crops. The population subsists primarily upon a grain diet, mostly wheat. Cotton in recent years has become increasingly important to industrial development, but must compete with wheat for suitable land. More than 500,000 tons of vegetables and a lesser amount of oil seeds are produced annually. In the past twenty years sugar, both beet and cane, has been grown in increasing amounts. The pride of Afghanistan's agriculture, however, comes from its orchards, melons, and vineyards (Table 1). Excellent varieties of apricots, peaches, plums, sweet melons, and grapes are grown throughout the country. Dried or fresh tree fruits and grapes are shipped to India and Pakistan. Yet for much of the year Afghans go without produce because preservation techniques are inadequate.

Animal husbandry is a large factor in the economy. Next to farming, the herding of sheep, goats, and cattle absorbs the largest portion of the labor force. Some two million nomads move their animals along annual routes from the plateaus into the mountains during the summer and back down again in the fall. Their progress follows the timetable of grass growth, but movement must be constant since the desert foliage burns off quickly in the late spring and the grasses are thin in the highest mountain valleys. Their paths cross not only topographical and climate frontiers; immemorially they have also traversed what are now international boundaries in search of feed and markets. In recent years increasing numbers of nomads appear to be making the transition to seminomadism and even to entirely sedentary farming.

The major purposes of stock raising are the production of wool, hides, cooking oil, dairy products, and meat. Some 15 million sheep are raised for their wool or to be slaughtered for their *roghan* (an oil from a sac under the tail of the fat-tailed sheep), hides, and their flesh. More important for export trade is karakul (Persian lamb). Government estimates put the number of karakul sheep slaughtered annually at 5.5 million. Most of their pelts are marketed in Western Europe or the United States.

Several million goats and about two million cattle provide dairy products; several hundreds of thousands of donkeys, camels, and horses serve as pack and work animals.

Between 85 and 90 per cent of the population depend upon raising crops or animals for a livelihood. This dependence suggests the rudimentary nature of the economy, yet Afghan nomads and cultivators are generally thought to enjoy a better diet than do their Indian or Pakistani counterparts. If true, this would appear to result from the low pressure of population and also from traditional Afghan skills in water use. Considerable increases in agricultural output also appear possible. Archeological evidence and historical literature confirm that Afghanistan supported a much denser and less agriculturally oriented population before the Mongol invasions of the thirteenth and fourteenth centuries. Cities far larger than any in modern Afghanistan (Balkh was reputed to have 800,000 residents at the time of its destruction by the Mongols) were supported by enormous irrigation systems in northern Afghanistan and probably also in the Helmand-Seistan regions. The contemporary dependence upon pastoralism and farming represents an economic regression which has persisted over the past six centuries. The countryside as a whole suffered a depopulation and the tribal organizations of nomads and seminomads came to dominate Afghan life.

Other Resources

While the surveying of Afghan minerals and energy resources is still in its infancy, recent discoveries make it clear that the country can support modest industrial development. The most important established minerals are coal, iron, natural gas, and lapis lazuli.

Coal reserves may run as high as several hundred million tons. They took on much greater potential importance with the discovery in the early 1960's of a major iron ore deposit about ninety miles west of Kabul. The ore is of high quality and the deposit is known to exceed two billion tons. Another discovery which may eventually contribute to iron and steel development is natural gas. It has been found in large deposits at Sheberghan, west of Mazar-i-Sharif. No readily exploitable oil has yet been found.

Lapis lazuli is a distinctive product of Afghanistan. The only major mine in the world is located in the northeastern province of Badakhshan. This semiprecious stone has been exported from the region since perhaps as early as 2500 B.C.

Recent mineral exploration has produced additional discoveries of gold, zinc, lead, barite, sulphur, tin, chromium, manganese, aluminum, mica, beryllium, and beryl. Some of these may prove to be economically exploitable, but most have been small amounts in remote areas.

Afghanistan has considerable potential for hydroelectric development. Its major rivers drop sharply, creating sufficient head for electric generation. With their relative accessibility and steady water flow throughout the year the Kabul and Kunduz rivers have been the easiest to develop.

The remoteness of the areas of greatest gravity fall in the Helmand, Hari Rud and Amu Darya basins inhibits comparable hydroelectric development, although multipurpose plans do exist for these rivers.

Despite this diversified assortment of mineral and energy resources, obstacles to rapid development are likely to be stubborn. Existing paved roads come reasonably close to major mineral sites only in the northern plain. More inhibiting are the present limitations on Afghanistan's market capacity to absorb the production of iron and steel at an economically feasible rate. There would be large expenses involved in transporting industrial products to Afghanistan's immediate neighbors. Moreover, there are social and cultural patterns within Afghan life which must undergo major transformations before advantage can be taken of large-scale industrial opportunities.

Location and Communications

Afghanistan's long history demonstrates that its location within Central Asia is a source of both strength and weakness. For long periods her crossroads position brought material and cultural wealth. From the northeast came the silk routes out of China which crossed Afghanistan's northern plains and moved through Persia toward the Mediterranean. Trade from India moved through the passes of eastern Afghanistan stopping at such convenient collection and refitting points as Kabul, Ghazni, and Bamian and then intersecting the northern route at Balkh. Some of these Indian products then moved westward, but others continued northward to Bokhara and Samarkand. An alternative route from India passed through Kandahar to Herat, avoiding the Hindu Kush. Afghanistan's largest cities thus are descendants of this long-term trade.

Afghan traders, merchants, bankers, and artisans appear to have gotten a large share of the income generated by Asian international trade prior to Vasco da Gama. After his voyage around the Cape of Good Hope, an increasingly larger percentage of goods from India, China, and other major producing centers in Asia was moved by ship. Afghanistan's trade declined sharply and by the early nineteenth century her cities had decayed physically and economically. Similar stagnation in her neighbors in the Middle East, Central Asia, and much of India throughout the eighteenth and nineteenth centuries deepened the malaise. Her inland location has also proved to be a serious disadvantage for modern economic growth. She is far from the original seats of commercial and industrial innovation, and neighbors have been barriers to the contact and trade which might have stimulated an earlier process of internal change.

The cities which serve as Afghanistan's points of contact with the outside world survived the long decline and have regained vitality in the twentieth century. In the east, Kabul is at the head of a system of roads which reach toward Pakistan and India. Kandahar is linked to the trade which moves through Quetta and Pakistani Baluchistan. Herat faces Meshed in eastern Iran. Mazar-i-Sharif is connected with two Russian ports on the Amu Darya, Khelif and Tormez. Qizil Qala serves as the port for the Kunduz Valley. Goods exchanged across the Amu are moved by river barge or steamer. Highways are responsible for the bulk of transfers in the other border regions. Camels and other pack animals move an undetermined share of goods through the more remote crossings. The lack of railways so far has not hindered foreign trade adequate for Afghan needs.

Ease of overland access has encouraged a long series of migrations which have created difficult challenges to national unity. Major ethnic groups straddle Afghanistan's borders in four directions: the Turks in the north, the Pushtuns in the east, the Baluchis in the south, and the Turkomans and other tribes in the west have intimate cultural and even kinship ties with their counterparts in the Soviet Union, Pakistan, or Iran. The annual movements of the nomads complicate the picture further. They have been accustomed to crossing all of the international frontiers in their quest for grazing land and trade. Afghanistan's terrain is harsh, but its location has permitted few natural frontiers, a legacy which has complicated the task of nation building.

Peoples

No comprehensive census has ever been taken in Afghanistan and there are wide differences of opinion on the size of the population. Estimates range from nine to fifteen million; the most persuasive evidence suggests between eleven and twelve million. There is general agreement that the urban population is somewhat less than one million and that two million persons live as permanent nomads.

History and setting have provided Afghanistan with a large variety of peoples and languages. The constant process of invasion and migration has produced much cultural and ethnic intermixing, several waves of religious conversions, episodic depopulations, and the marooning of a variety of survivors from earlier times in inaccessible pockets. As a result, today there are at least thirty distinct languages native to Afghanistan. These are spread among four major language families, although the Iranian tongues are by far the most widely known. Approximately one-half of the population speaks Pushtu. Its speakers are limited for the most part to the Pushtun tribes in eastern Afghanistan. Farsi (Persian) is more widely used. It is the mother tongue of perhaps one-third of the population, but is commonly spoken as a second language in all regions. Several other Iranian languages are spoken by isolated mountain communities. Baluchi, spoken by the nomads of the Registan Desert, is also of Iranian origin.

Related to these Iranian languages is the Dardic group found in some of the most remote valleys of northeast Afghanistan. Here small tribal groups persist whose cultural ancestry may possibly be traced beyond Alexander the Great to the original Indo-Iranian migrants who may have entered Afghanistan before 2000 B.C.

Speakers of Turkish languages are concentrated in an arc across northern Afghanistan from the Khirghiz of the Wakhan Corridor in the far east to the Turkomans of the Maimana region of the northwest. The number of Turkish speakers is estimated to be somewhat more than one million.

Traces of two other language families are found. Arabic is the native language of a few thousand villagers in the northern plain. And in the far south, Brahui survives, a language related to the Dravidian group of south India.

Ethnic Groups

There are several major groups within Afghanistan to whom Afghans themselves impute racial characteristics. While there are measurable differences among these

groups in heredity, language, culture, physical characteristics, and historical experience, they also have a great deal
in common. Practically all of Afghanistan's ethnic groups
have similar occupational patterns and their life styles,
mostly as farmers and herders, are essentially the same.
Thus, while distinctions persist and the psychological significance of perceptions of difference is important, it is
possible to exaggerate the importance of ethnic differences.

The Pushtuns have been the most numerous and politically dominant group in recent Afghan history. They account for about half of the population. Originally the term
"Afghan" referred only to the Pushtun tribes.

The origin of the Pushtuns is obscure. Their homeland
was the valleys of the Sulaiman Mountains of eastern Afghanistan. References to their mountaineer toughness,
love of combat, and jealousy of reputation have been consistent throughout their reported history. Invaders moving
through Afghanistan in order to reach the plains of northern India frequently had difficulty forcing the passes of
the Pushtun region. The fame of the dangerous Khyber
Pass for the invader or traveler is symbolic of Pushtun
hostility to strangers. Yet it appears that Pushtun relations
with foreigners were primarily defensive until the Islamic
invasions of north India began shortly before 1000 A.D.
From that time the Pushtuns have been emerging from
their former homeland, moving eastward into the Indus
Valley and westward into much of the rest of modern
Afghanistan. This process may have been accelerated by
the destruction of the agricultural and urban centers of
the Helmand-Seistan region during the invasions of the
Mongols and Tamerlane.

It is likely that the Pushtun inheritance is mixed. There

are a variety of physical characteristics among them: in skin color they range from fair to dark copper or brown, and in hair color from reddish to nearly black, and in eye color from occasional blue or gray to deep brown. However, nearly all have a light, sinewy physique. The complexity of their inheritance is also suggested by the large number of tribal units into which they are divided. Of perhaps ten major Pushtun tribes, the two largest and most powerful are the Durranis (also known as Abdalis) and the Ghilzais.

The clearest unifying features of Pushtun life are cultural. Their social system, social code, and sense of common history tend to draw them together more effectively than do ethnic considerations. Largely responsible for this sense of brotherhood is the set of values associated with the code of Pushtunwali. Its influence has been so pervasive in Pushtun life that in most respects it governs attitude and behavior more completely than does Islam's basic set of laws, the Shariah.

Highest in the priorities of values established in the Pushtunwali is fearlessness in combat. Pushtun tribes and clans have been organized pre-eminently for struggle against nature and the outsider, whether he be Pushtun or not. The barren terrain of most of eastern Afghanistan induced Pushtuns to seek a large part of their livelihood from plunder or conquest. Attitudes bred in this competitive environment ensured incessant conflict. Hence the emphasis that Pushtunwali places upon warrior values.

Important corollaries to the demand for valor are the values given to cooperation, chivalry, honor, honesty, and pride. Elaborate rules apply to the conduct of war and the settlement leading to peace. Crucial to Pushtun acceptance of justifiable violence is the emphasis given to righteous revenge (*badal*). This concept is responsible for intra- and inter-tribal feuds, many of which may last for several generations.

Softening this belief in "an eye for an eye" have been the democratic and chivalrous elements built into the code. Tribal members, unless suffering from some social disability, have a potent voice in determining policies and justice under the leadership of established chiefs. Through the institutions of the jirga, or council, Pushtuns have worked for in-group harmony and consensus. Moreover in a barren environment filled with human threats, great value has been placed upon hospitality. This obligation is even extended to asylum and protection for erstwhile enemies when they request it.

Tying together the requirements of Pushtunwali is the sense of nobility attributed to those who observe it. A highly developed sense of honor is associated with the tribesman who complies with its strenuous demands and who achieves, in addition, the respect associated with piety. Based as it is upon close and vital interactions between tightly woven in-groups, Pushtunwali has contributed to the integrity and persistence of tribal institutions.

Pushtuns overwhelmingly control Afghanistan's modern political institutions. The royal family descends from one of the major Durrani clans. Most of the critical political and bureaucratic positions are filled by fellow Pushtuns, if not by fellow clansmen. This dominance has not, however, gone unchallenged in several important areas of Afghan life. Pushtuns do not have a monopoly over the economy, religious institutions, or some of the strongest of the surviving cultural traditions which are essential to Afghan nationalism.

The second most numerous ethnic group in Afghanistan is the Tajiks. As with the Pushtuns their origin is subject to debate. Most authorities believe them to be Iranian, but when and under what circumstances they might have settled in Afghanistan remains unknown. Throughout recorded history the great majority of Tajiks have been sedentary cultivators or townsmen. They have populated the most extensive and fertile valleys and have built most of the cities. They form the great majority of Afghans who are native speakers of Persian and they are the only large ethnic group which is not tribally organized.

While responsible for a large share of Afghanistan's material and cultural wealth, the Tajiks have been continuously overrun by intruders. The Pushtuns are only the last of a long series of conquerors to seize, pillage, tax, and govern them. Estimates generally place their portion of the population at 30 per cent.

More assertive, but less numerous than the Tajiks, are the Turko-Mongols of northern Afghanistan. They descend jointly from Mongol and Turkish forebears, but history has split them into several distinct communities. Most numerous in Afghanistan are the Uzbeks who may number nearly one million. Mazar-i-Sharif is their major urban center, but the majority of Uzbeks are spread across the northern plain from Kunduz to Maimana as farmers and seminomads.

In the far northwest some 200,000 to 300,000 Turkomans, many of whom are emigrées from the Russian Revolution, live a largely nomadic life. Known for their excellent horsemanship, Turkomans and Uzbeks raise the major share of Afghan karakul.

Much smaller groups of Turko-Mongols inhabit the Badakhshan and Wakhan regions of northeastern Afghan-

..stan. There a few tens of thousands of Khirghiz and Kazaks, some of whom are also refugees from Soviet Russia, eke out their existence in Afghanistan's highest valleys.

One other group of Turks has been historically, if not numerically, important. The Qizil Bashes descend from Turkish mercenary troops brought into Afghanistan during the seventeenth and eighteenth centuries by Persian conquerors. Afghan kings subsequently used them as elite troops. They continue as city dwellers, many of whom have taken up crafts or administrative careers.

The Hazaras are the most alien and most remote of the major ethnic groups in Afghanistan. With broad heads, often strong Mongoloid features, and short sturdy physiques the Hazaras have been considered and treated by the Pushtuns as inferiors, fit only for hard labor. Probably descended from Mongol invaders, Tajiks, and other peoples, the Hazaras until recently were confined to the inhospitable region of the central and western Hindu Kush known as the Hazarajat. Estimates of their number vary from 500,000 to 1,000,000. Since the mid-1950's they have been migrating to Kabul and other cities to work as laborers.

Minor and often exotic groups are also found in the more remote areas of Afghanistan. Most notable of these are the Nuristanis or Kafirs of the higher valleys of the Hindu Kush east of Kabul. These people were conquered and converted by the Afghan government in the 1890's. The frequent incidence of blue eyes, redheads, and even blonds among them, and their generally Mediterranean appearance, has led to many inconclusive speculations about their origin.

Other ethnic groups include the nomadic Baluchis of Registan and several important tribal groups of mixed descent generically known as the Chahar Aimak (Four Tribes) who inhabit the regions surrounding Herat. Foreign settler groups have also had some importance. For centuries a small Jewish community has played a significant banking and commercial role, principally in Kabul. Also, perhaps 50,000 Indians, most of them Sikhs, are concentrated in Kabul or nearby towns, usually as shopkeepers.

Afghanistan's physical and human setting provides imposing obstacles to the establishment of unified authority and common standards of national life and culture. While the countryside is endowed with promising mineral and energy resources, Afghanistan's location and the wide scattering of its population have made economic integration difficult. On the other hand the environment has helped produce tough and tenacious people. The scarcity of food and fodder has bred the qualities of mobility, stamina, and independence into most of the major ethnic groups. Despite their technological and cultural limitations, Afghan tribes have learned to act upon values which assured their survival. In few areas of the world have traditions been more persistently maintained than in isolated Afghan valleys.

Pushtunwali values which have promoted survival and the qualities of honor and dignity inevitably offer resistance to the types of changes essential for a viable national society. The parochialisms of the family, clan, tribe, linguistic or ethnic group, or of a valley or region stand in the way of closer identity with the symbols and needs of a nation. These barriers are at least partially softened by overlapping patterns of identity which gave Afghanistan an incipient sense of community before modern times. The use of Persian as a common language among almost all groups and the acceptance of Islam by 99 per cent of the population provided preconditions for a sense of nationality. Furthermore, whatever their ethnic, historical, or linguistic differences, the lives of most Afghans were culturally quite similar. A diet based upon wheat, irrigation techniques needed to grow that wheat, dependence upon sheep raising, constant reliance upon similar tactics of defense and attack, acceptance of tribal structures and leadership, and insistence upon individual dignity are inheritances common to most Afghans. Throughout their history these practices and attitudes have led to incessant conflict among them. Now with the introduction of nationalist ideas, a growing number of these features have come to be considered worth fighting for on behalf of a unified community.

Social Characteristics

Narrowness of view and capacity to survive are mutually reinforcing traits of Afghan cultural life. The tenacious survival of village and tribal communities in the face of constant invasion, severe climate, and often barren soil can be attributed primarily to compact and inward-looking social institutions. Although this parochialism has hindered the transformation of Afghanistan into a modern society, there are features in the culture, especially those attitudes which encourage cooperation, shared responsibility, and reciprocal obligations which may prove to be increasingly applicable to modernization.

The limited horizons of Afghan interests, tastes, and values are functions of the intense and localized social units which govern traditional life. Primary loyalty is to family, clan, tribe, and perhaps village and religious sect. Family loyalty stands first, and the relative importance given to other social units depends upon a variety of shifting considerations. Observations concerning these social institutions must be tentative; little investigation of their complex and pluralistic structure has been undertaken.

Virtually every type of Afghan community is based upon a clearly defined social unit. Personal ambitions, interests, responsibilities, and, to a large extent, abilities are most often identified with family membership. Individuals rarely behave without reference to a complex set of relationships that tie them to their closest kin. Social mobility is restricted because the ability or capacity of an individual to take advantage of unprecedented opportunities can be offset by the needs or desires of other family members. Family ties instead tend to produce nepotism. Advancement achieved by an able family member is expected to result in greater opportunities for his relatives. Family reputation and pride must figure largely in the shaping of individual ambitions; since family identity is tenacious, feuds and rivalries between families can have far-reaching impact on behavior.

Afghan families are the fundamental economic and political units within the culture. Consequently, patterns of wealth in land and livestock, of prestige in courage and wisdom, and power in retainers and guns depend ultimately upon family structure. This dependence also governs attitudes on social and sexual relationships. Women are often seen as instruments of exchange by which family power and status may be strengthened. The cementing of alliances with relatives tends to produce endogamous marriages even to the point of uniting first cousins. However, while the Afghan family is an effective instrument for holding, enjoying, and transmitting wealth, its biological and social purposes have been achieved at the price of constricting Afghan cultural perspectives. This narrowing influence is amplified by the family's educational and recreational functions, both of which tend to reinforce inward-looking attitudes.

The clan and tribal dimensions of Afghan life offer wider arenas for experience and outlook, but their functions generally overlap those of the family. Despite rivalry between the family units within clans and tribes, these larger groups also promote outlets for individual expression and the means of economic and social security.

Within the towns and villages dominated by the Tajiks, the family remains the basic social unit, although village-level institutions or occupational guilds often play important institutional roles. Spatial isolation also ensures that the social horizon of most villagers and townsmen does not reach far beyond their valley or the surrounding mountain ridges.

Nomads and merchants generally accumulate wider contacts than does the peasant majority of the population. By definition, the nomads are acquainted with a variety of communities and regions. Interaction with peasants is vital to them. It makes possible the exchange of grain and other food for animal products. Nomads also often serve as the source of supply for manufactured goods in the more remote regions. Consequently, they are also disseminators of cultural innovations in the villages. Such relationships, while frequently subject to friction, are an enduring feature of Afghan life. Each group depends upon the other, but rarely does either adopt the ways of the other. Thus while innovation is a possible result of nomadic contact, relatively little intimacy or exchange of habits and skills has occurred.

The small minority of merchants and artisans, who are concentrated in the towns or larger villages, also serve as focal points of social interaction. Their influence, however, is limited largely because they constitute a small and often alien element in the population. Moreover, the political power monopolized by peasant and nomad groups on the basis of tribal organization has restricted artisan and merchant influence.

Afghan views of Islam have also tended to limit mental horizons. Religious leaders have played a crucial role in this respect. While there is no organized system which determines the power and influence of the mullahs or ulema, they are the primary source of education and moral attitudes for most Afghans. There is no cohesive system for the education, training, placement, promotion, or expulsion of religious specialists. Their leadership is largely a function of the personal qualities of learning, piety, and guidance possessed by individual mullahs. The absence of a centralized structure has meant that religious leadership in Afghanistan is almost wholly governed by local factors. This provincialization of ecclesiastical experience and attitudes tends to be reflected by the laymen within their congregations.

Religion in Afghanistan also contributes to narrowness of experience and attitude because of the strongly puritanical interpretation given Islam by most mullahs. The faith emphasizes clear-cut rules of behavior whose purpose is mainly to purify and reinforce the faith of the believer. To a large extent this is accomplished through rigidly accepted prohibitions in diet, speech, and behavior. In Afghanistan negative injunctions have been extended further, especially to purdah, the restriction of women from public activity. Generally, puritanical attitudes are reinforced by the other factors which divide Afghan society into exclusive groups. With a wide variety of rules whose observation determines individual piety and worth, there are nearly limitless opportunities for invidious comparisons between the moral standards of one tribe and another, one village and another, or one region and another.

These parochial traits have been amplified by the overall pattern of Afghan experience throughout history. One characteristic of Afghan history has been continual invasion. While there have been opportunities to learn from foreign influences, conflict with intruders has distorted or limited cultural exchanges. Such experience has increased Afghan isolation, yet pressure from the outside has not produced a sense of unity and interdependence as might be expected from the defense of a common homeland. Invasions have often divided the region politically and usually have added new cultural groups which must be accommodated. Thus, they have tended to separate further the largely autonomous units of the society.

While Afghan life and its viewpoints and institutions have been segmented, it is obvious that they have not lost their vitality. Perhaps because the social system has been divided into small and often hostile and competing groups, a composite culture has been able to survive. In almost all aspects Afghan culture is based upon institutional and technological complexes which are small in scale. The patterns of life in the tribe, village, and town are limited to a small range of skills and sets of beliefs. More elaborate structures, large urban and agro-irrigational systems perished, for example, while life based upon parochial units and localized irrigation and nomadism stubbornly persisted.

Traditions of cooperation within these small units have contributed to their survival. Cooperation and consensus are fundamental features of tribal polity. This is most dramatically demonstrated by the significance of the tribal council, the jirga. Partially offsetting the authority of the chiefs and the rivalries between families, the jirga has developed as an instrument of defense, organization, and harmony in tribal life. The structure and authority of the council varies with local traditions and experience. Its most basic feature is the acceptance of the principle that all family interests within the group concerned may be represented in deliberations of justice, war, labor, and land. The spirit and procedure are usually democratic. Theoretically, a consensus of the whole group in question is necessary, if it is to act. The jirga therefore encourages a considerable degree of individual initiative, although in many instances it may be dominated by powerful chiefs. It is also a convenient device for accommodation among competing interests. As an instrument of government, the jirga offers intriguing possibilities for contemporary social and political integration in Afghanistan. There is no traditional limit to the size of the group to which the jirga principle might be applied. Within the clan or small tribe it is usually composed of ordinary tribesmen. Among large tribes or tribal confederations, which could occasionally include nearly all of the Pushtun population, a jirga might consist of tribal chiefs (khans) or clan leaders (*maliks*) representing their communities.

The jirga has been applied on a national basis with increasing frequency in the twentieth century. The convocation of several Loya, or national, jirgas, has been integral to the effort to build a modern Afghan national state. Thus while parochialism has been the prevalent characteristic of Afghan society, consensus offers a partially compensating tradition which may provide a vital element in the building of a common sense of Afghan citizenship.

Islam in Afghanistan

Virtually all Afghans are Muslim. There is a sprinkling of native Jews and Hindus, but they account for little more than 1 per cent of the population. Perhaps four-fifths of the Muslims are of the Sunna or orthodox sect. Most of the remaining Muslims are of the Shiah, Islam's most numerous minority sect. Tempered by the conditions of isolation and social fragmentation, Islam is the strongest unifying cultural force within Afghan society.

Few religious institutions in Afghanistan have elaborate organization. The primary functional units are mosques for congregational worship; schools for predominantly religious education; and special centers of learning and piety which are often associated with mosques, monasteries, or shrines. Leadership, administration, and financing are locally based, with the exceptions of large pilgrimage centers and the religious charities which are supported by the central government. Individual mullahs subsist upon fees for ceremonial and advisory services on behalf of their clients and often receive endowments of land or agricultural income from the villages or tribes who engage them.

Many mullahs cultivate or at least oversee their own land. The support of corporate institutions such as schools, mosques, and monasteries has traditionally come from endowments based upon land—the concept of wakf. Customarily, the mullahs have managed this income on their own behalf. Pilgrimage centers and some of the higher-level schools (madrasahs) collect fees from pilgrims and students.

The great majority of Afghanistan's religious specialists concentrate upon teaching and the conduct of prayer and other public ceremonies for their livelihood. A smaller group, which maintains a tradition of greater intellectual sophistication, enforces Islamic laws. The two most important positions which they have occupied for this purpose have been those of the kazi, or judge, and the mufti, his assistant in interpreting religious law. Authority to determine guilt, rights, and justice, even within secular affairs, has often been lodged with religious specialists from whom there has been little effective appeal.

This decentralization of judicial authority is reflected by the tendency of Afghan jurists to mix the strictures of domestic tribal codes, most notably Pushtunwali, with the more abstract codes of the Islamic legal system. The treatment of serious crimes is frequently based upon tribal mores which accept revenge and restitution through blood or money payments. Customary attitudes toward the role of women tend to push aside basic Islamic principles so that Afghan women have weaker civil rights than are established in the Shariah.

The secular activities of the clergy supplement the prestige and authority they gain from their professional roles. If their individual reputation for wisdom is outstanding, laymen frequently depend upon their advice over a range of practical matters, some of which touch upon the structure of power within the immediate community. Being in constant personal contact with their congregations, mullahs often mold opinion on questions of property, propriety, and reputation.

While the worldly functions of the mullahs bring them a large share of wealth and prestige, greatest religious respect is reserved for otherworldly figures, or pirs, who give up participation in the ordinary affairs of men. They are supported by charity and concentrate their efforts upon developing total and pure faith in Allah. In pursuing this goal many pirs have been associated with the traditions of Sufi mysticism. Their saintliness has often become the basis for Afghan cults which, while consistent with Islam, may also be amalgamated with local folk beliefs. Many mosques and shrines have been built over the tombs of the most illustrious of these saints.

Afghan religion, therefore, is a mixture of highly sophisticated theological concepts and the most localized, sometimes animistic, beliefs of remote peasants and nomads. Islam's message and standards reach deeply into the character of all groups in the population. To some extent its influence is pervasive because its tenets have been permitted to mingle with local cults. A major accomplishment of Afghanistan's religious leaders has been meditation between and combination of these two religious traditions. Nevertheless, the decentralization of judicial authority largely in the hands of the ulema presents serious obstacles to the concentration of effective government authority.

Traditional Patterns of Power and Wealth

Few rules apply across the spectrum of tribal and other forms of socio-political organization in Afghanistan. All tribes have leaders usually known as khans, but the manner of their selection and the extent of their power varies widely. Some tribes are almost completely controlled by khans who hold much of the tribal wealth and who may treat ordinary tribesmen as serfs or tenant farmers. In other circumstances the distribution of power may be nearly egalitarian. Khans may be elected on the basis of consensus within a tribal jirga and the distribution of wealth may be periodically reallocated in order to ensure that all families possess roughly equal shares. Among the Pushtun tribes which have remained in their homeland there tends to be relatively little socio-economic distance between khans and tribesmen. Away from their home region there is a tendency for the power of the chieftain to increase at the expense of the commoner. This gulf is especially obvious in the Kunduz, Herat, and Farah regions. Some of the khans in these areas hold large estates and assign tenants or laborers to work their land. To some extent this is also true of areas near Kabul and Kandahar where some of the most powerful members of the Durrani and Ghilzai tribes own large estates.

This concentration of political and economic power cuts across ethnic divisions. Thus Tajik landlords might employ Tajiks and other groups on their lands near Herat, while in many areas Pushtun khans employ Pushtuns, Hazaras, Tajiks, Uzbeks, and others. On the other hand, egalitarian communities of small farms can be found usually in the remoter mountain valleys among most of the major ethnic groups.

To a large extent, the pattern of relative degrees of wealth and power determines the quality of social relationships within the tribes. But even where power is monopolized, the Pushtun code requires that all full members of the tribe, even if many are actually tenants, must be treated with respect. This reflects the relative recentness of the expansion of Pushtun control under strong chiefs over areas of northern, western, and southwestern Afghanistan. The tradition of the egalitarian tribe has partially survived recent seizures of land and the establishment of large estates.

Even the more democratically organized tribes often employ separate ethnic groups as tenants or laborers. Within the original Pushtun area many of the tribes dominate client peoples known as Hamsayas. These clients hold traditionally protected positions. They have no say in the direction of over-all tribal affairs, but their economic rights and physical security are guaranteed by the tribal members whose standard of living usually is not markedly higher than that of the Hamsayas.

Economic as well as social differences between members of the nomad tribes also tend to be small. While some chiefs possess very large herds of sheep, cattle, or camels, there generally is little economic distance between nomads. The sense of shared representative leadership within these moving tribes is generally stronger than among the sedentary groups.

Tribal organization is largely founded upon the rationale of the necessity for common defense and is held together by alliances of families and clans and by participation in the jirga. The integrity of the tribal structure requires considerable give and take on divisions of power and wealth. Such circumstances cause even the most powerful of families to treat weaker neighbors with caution.

Class Relations

In contemporary Afghanistan the most important class relationship is that between landlord and cultivator. The significance of this for the tribal structure has been suggested. The gulf between landlord and tenant often parallels ethnic divisions. Pushtuns are the most prominent employers of other peoples, but there are Tajik, Hazara, and Turkish landlords in regions where these groups are dominant. Relationships between landlords and tenants vary greatly according to origin of the connection and upon the realities of competition for labor and for land. Some relationships reflect the control of one group by another for several centuries. For the most part the historical basis of extensive landowning appears to have come from conquest after which the subjugated people have been allowed a share of the crops from the land which they originally owned.

Division of the crops between landlord and tenant or laborer is determined by relative contributions and bargaining leverage. Rent is often one-half or more of the gross crop. Tenants who contribute all elements of capital and labor may be able to keep 60 per cent. The question of security of tenure is vital. Tenants and laborers protected by long-standing traditional arrangements generally are more secure, but in regions where land has changed hands recently and where large numbers of cultivators must compete for land, their bargaining power is limited; often they are forced to annual contracts. Insecurity of tenure especially afflicts the cultivators in the larger river valleys and in regions where new commercial crops have been introduced.

The emergence of commercial agriculture which re-
places subsistence consumption of the crop with transfers
to an outside market has generally weakened the traditional bonds of reciprocal obligations between landlords
and tenants. In the traditional relationship tenants were
frequently considered to be the retainers and followers of
their landlords The landlord's obligations toward them
included protection and the provision of necessities in
emergencies. Increasing commercialization in some of the
more fertile valleys has tended to convert this personal relationship into one that is primarily economic.

Other class relationships include those between nomad
and peasant, and townsman and farmer or herder. Men-
tion has been made of the mutually dependent relationship between peasant and nomad. When the relationship
is in balance, exchanges of grain for animal products are
usually mutually satisfactory. In recent years, however,
there has been increasing rivalry for land between these
two classes. As nomads find some of their traditional movements and sources of livelihood cut off from them by modern developments like the closing of the Russian or Pakistani borders and the absorption of camel caravan traffic
by highway trucking, they have increasingly had to compete for available land. Among cultivators whose socioeconomic organization is weak or who are small in number,
there has been a tendency to succumb to Pushtun nomadic
control, often through money lending. This trend continues to develop in the Hazarajat, although the major
Hazara tribes appear to be resisting it effectively.

Until as recently as forty years ago most Afghan merchant and artisan groups were in a state of decline or
stagnation. Constant political turmoil in the eighteenth
and nineteenth centuries and Afghanistan's loss of inter-

national trade had destroyed the basis of their earlier prosperity. In large part the process by which Pushtun tribesmen have built a national government has been accomplished by the conquest of towns, which had previously been controlled by merchants and artisans. The result has been not only a loss of urban political influence, but the collapse of organization, skills, and economic activity. Their markets constricted and they suffered from plundering and heavy taxation imposed by tribally and rurally oriented rulers. The operations of merchants and artisans were no longer based upon independence of purpose or structure. Kandahar and Jalalabad are the classic examples of cities organized by tribesmen for tribal needs, with merchants and artisans only serving auxiliary roles. Urban groups in Herat and Kabul have been permitted by tradition and circumstances to enjoy greater autonomy, but the picture presented until the late nineteenth century was that of dying urban communities. The subsistence orientation of the peasant and nomad made them virtually independent of the towns economically, while their numbers and organization gave them political control of both town and countryside.

This cursory analysis of some of the leading features of Afghan society suggests how little is known about its dynamics. At many points the integrity and fabric of traditional Afghan social relations are under mounting pressure to change. Whether the essence and spirit of Afghan life, especially its democratic elements and its genuine religiosity, will persist in this new type of struggle for survival will largely be determined by the resiliency of its attitudes and institutions.

2. Historical Setting: The Struggle for Unity and Independence

The creation of a viable state and the assertion of Afghan nationality are recent events posed against a long history. Political consolidation can be traced only to the early eighteenth century. This process which produced a state from a loosely related group of tribes remains largely unstudied, but the major accomplishments which were required for political unity are clear.

Events before the eighteenth century bear little resemblance to subsequent developments, especially with regard to politics. Afghanistan had been periodically subjected to invasions, migrations, and frequent shifts of political jurisdiction. These events added to the variety of communities and cultures, but rarely, if at all, did the region experience political, economic, or even a cultural unity. Consequently, the concept of nationhood had virtually no chance of developing until long after such polities as England, Spain, Japan, Korea, or Thailand had begun to mature. The building of a nation has required the refocusing of political and cultural attitudes as much as it has meant the mobilization and centralization of power.

Early Influences

The list of peoples and conquerors who have touched or influenced Afghan history reads like a roster of nearly every aggressive force that has been set loose in Asia over the past 4,000 years. The Indo-Aryans are the first people recorded to have invaded the region, probably before the sixteenth century B.C. They were followed by the Persians, who conquered most of the region in the sixth century B.C. Two centuries later, Alexander the Great marched through leaving several colonies manned by his Greek mercenaries. Their descendants built a semi-Greek culture in Bactria. Shortly thereafter they were overwhelmed by a series of invaders from the Central Asian steppes. Among these, the Kushans left the deepest mark. They built an empire which included most of northern India and Central Asia and lasted for nearly 400 years. During this era Buddhism was introduced. Cities and trade flourished in the north, and in the Kabul and Peshawar regions a sophisticated aesthetic tradition, the Gandharan, largely inspired by Hellenistic techniques and themes produced remarkable painting, sculpture, and architecture.

Buddhist monasteries and urban centers survived the onslaught of an invasion by the Huns in the fourth and fifth centuries A.D. For several centuries thereafter minor kings or chieftains, some under the influence of the Iranian Sassanian dynasty, divided up the region.

Islam was the next vitalizing factor. It was carried primarily by Turkish armies from the sultanates of Central Asia. Their most significant accomplishment was the creation of the Muslim state of Ghazni in 961. Under the leadership of Mahmud, its greatest sultan, Ghazni became the capital of an empire which dominated most of Central and western Asia and northern India. An elaborate court and intellectual life developed with the employment of many of the most eminent Muslim scientists, historians, poets, philosophers, and engineers of the era.

Mahmud's unbroken line of victories could not be maintained after his death in 1030 and his dynasty slowly declined. It was replaced by the Ghurids of western Afghanistan who may have been Tajiks. Their generals were able to conquer northern India early in the thirteenth century, but new waves of Turkish invaders destroyed their Afghan base almost at the same time.

The following century was perhaps the most disastrous ever experienced by the region. Beginning with the campaigns of Genghis Khan four generations of Mongols conquered, plundered, and massacred. One result was the destruction of the large irrigation systems which had supported the sophisticated culture of Balkh, the middle Helmand Valley, Herat, and Ghazni. The sacking and depopulation of these regions broke the continuity of cultural life which had extended backwards to the Kushan era.

Partial restoration of the region's earlier life was achieved by the descendants of Timur (Tamerlane) after he had ravaged the remaining urban and agricultural centers. His son, Shah Rukh, supported the rebuilding of Herat with forts, schools, and mosques and encouraged a remarkable artistic revival.

Nearly three centuries of settlement in Central Asia domesticated the Mongols. Babur (1483–1530), the scion of one of their princely families, used the Kabul region as the base for yet another conquest of India. He swept the Indo-Gangetic plain to establish the Mughul Empire in 1526. His successors built its enormous power with Indian resources (and Central Asian manpower) and until the late seventeenth century it also held much of Afghanistan.

Mughul claims to the area did not go uncontested. In the sixteenth century, Uzbeks began to move across the Amu Darya into the northern plains. More potent, however, was the challenge of Safawid Persia which had seized and held Herat and the lower Helmand region. Three times in the seventeenth century Kandahar changed hands.

While these conquerors vied for its most prosperous sections, a process more significant for Afghanistan's future was beginning. Spurred by religious revivalism, the Pushtun tribes became increasingly conscious of their cultural unity. The campaigns of foreign imperial armies and their demands for taxes and submission stimulated Pushtun resistance. During the late seventeenth century this was directed toward the Mughuls. The outstanding figure of this struggle was Khushlal Khan Khattak (1613–1689), a Pushtun tribal leader renowned for his valor and for the rhetoric of his appeal for Pushtun unity. His poetry of war and of the romance of Pushtun life established much of the foundation for Pushtu literature. The guerrilla struggle was largely successful. Early in the eighteenth century most of the Pushtun region asserted its autonomy.

The Persians were also driven out. Under Ghilzai leadership, Kandahar was seized from the Safawids in 1709. In an attempt to control the tribes, the Persians had forced a large section of the Durranis to migrate to Herat. In 1716 they also rebelled and helped to expel the Persians.

During the next few years an explosion of Ghilzai power occurred. They destroyed the shaken Safawid Empire and captured Isfahan, its capital, in 1722. Over the next seven years Pushtuns controlled most of Iran, but they did not have the resources or the sophistication to make the conquest permanent. Led by the last of the great Central Asian horseback conquerors, Nadir Shah Afshar, the Persians rallied, threw out the Ghilzais, and reconquered Afghanistan. This conquest also proved temporary. Nadir was assassinated in 1747. His empire disintegrated and the political forces within Afghanistan were once again free to assert themselves.

As had been a common Persian practice, Nadir Shah had recruited Pushtun chieftains and their followers into his army. Among these was Ahmad Khan of the Sadozai clan of the Durrani tribe. In the course of Nadir's campaigns, Ahmad Khan rose to high rank. Chaos within the Persian army following the assassination gave him the opportunity to lead the Afghan forces back to their homeland. He was able to fill the political vacuum by winning Pushtun acceptance to his claims of leadership over all the tribes. In the process of making good on this claim, signified by his assumption of the title of Shah, he created the political vehicle for modern Afghan unity and independence.

Building the Afghan State, 1747–1880

Sadozai claims to royal ascendancy under Ahmad Shah were subject to challenge from the beginning. Several tribes were more powerful than the forces at Ahmad Shah's command. He was unable to demand the forms of submission from Pushtun leaders which could give him effective control. His task and that of his successors was primarily to win the obedience and acceptance of the jealously autonomous Afghan tribes by making them subject to the king as the paramount military power, the dispenser of justice, and the collector of taxes. In these matters the Afghan kings were to make uncertain progress until shortly before the twentieth century.

There were other obstacles to political unity. Effective control required changes in the parochial mentality of the tribes and solutions to the problem of communications over a region where major centers were days and sometimes seasons apart. The economy had suffered severely from centuries of constant warfare and also from the increasing diversion of Asian trade from inland to ocean routes. The cities were declining, the artisans and merchants were leaving or losing their skills and capital. Afghanistan also was insulated from the changing Islamic culture of Western Asia. This was partially the result of the sectarian rivalry between the Shiite Persians and the predominantly Sunni Afghans. The Persians stood between the Afghans and their cosectarians in the Ottoman Empire.

As a consequence of these limitations on their position, Afghan kings were rarely certain of political support from the major Pushtun tribes, had few resources which they could tap from the impoverished Tajiks and other minorities, and had little acquaintance with the techniques which governments were using elsewhere to build modern states. Moreover, by the early nineteenth century serious threats to Afghan independence were posed by the British in India and the Russians in Central Asia. After 1815, rivalry between Britain and Russia became the framework in which Afghan diplomacy had to be practiced. As armies and railroads moved toward Afghanistan, chances for its continued independence became increasingly doubtful. The prospects were not improved by the decline in the internal position of the monarchy after the death of Ahmad Shah's son and successor, Timur, in 1793. For a generation Sadozai princes fought inconclusively for the throne. Major regions broke away from royal control. The struggle for power degenerated into blood feuds with tribes and factions taking advantage of anarchy to reassert their freedom to pay off old scores.

A path out of this chaos was found under the leadership of Dost Mohammed, a Durrani prince of the Mohammedzai family and the Barakzai clan. After achieving effective control over most of eastern Afghanistan he took the title of amir in 1835. His attempt to consolidate control over the rest of the country was interrupted by the British invasion of 1839. After two years of frustration which led to military disaster, the British retired, permitting Dost Mohammed to resume his efforts to unify the country. By the end of his reign he controlled all the major provinces and had forced tribal acceptance of his leadership. He established the rudiments of a centrally recruited national army and was even able to cooperate with the British. The Afghan loss of Peshawar and the rest of their former Indian possessions, however, limited the degree of friendship.

Dost Mohammed's death in 1863 triggered yet another struggle for control. His third son, Shere Ali, prevailed in 1869 and ruled effectively until he was driven out by the British in their second invasion in 1879. Shere Ali continued his father's policies and was able to introduce some military and educational innovations. Modern foundries and workshops were established at Kabul. His plans for greater unification of the country through improved administration and communications were frustrated by weaknesses in the taxation system and Anglo-Russian intrusions.

British and Russian Interference

From the 1820's, after they had conquered most of India, the British became increasingly concerned about the potential threat of Russian expansion toward the Indus Valley; by the 1830's this rivalry had brought the two powers into conflict over Afghanistan. The major concern of each was to insure that their territories would not be threatened by hostile control over the Hindu Kush and its system of passes and trade routes. Eventually, Afghanistan came to serve as a buffer area separating the British and Russian forces from direct contact. Unfortunately, this arrangement developed at the cost of seriously disrupting the embryonic Afghan political system.

The British were the first to intervene. They fought the 1839–1842 war on the theory that control over Afghan affairs was the best assurance of Indian defense. Inability to control the Pushtun tribes soon convinced them that internal control of Afghanistan was either impossible or too costly; afterwards they were willing to recognize and support whichever prince gained the upper hand in Afghan politics.

A second aspect of British Afghan policy came from their need to control the Pushtun tribes living in the eastern valleys of the Sulaiman Mountains who constantly raided the Punjab plains. The British attempted to support the amirs in return for Kabul's cooperation in the pacification of these frontier tribes. This goal produced a conflict in objectives between the two governments. The amirs depended upon the eastern Pushtuns for internal defense of their thrones. British demands for the prohibition of tribal raids into India forced the amirs to choose between two sources of support.

There was much disagreement among the British on how to handle the situation. From the 1850's to the middle 1870's, the prevailing view was that the Afghan government should be supported and the tribes lightly supervised. However, alarm over the Russian conquests in Central Asia caused the British to adopt a "forward policy" aimed at insuring that at least the strategically valuable parts of Afghanistan would be defended. This required British military advisers in Afghan Turkistan and Herat and led to demands that Afghan foreign policy come completely under British control. Shere Ali was caught in the middle. His attempts to maintain neutrality were interpreted as hostile by the British and they attacked once again in 1879.

After a year of costly occupation during which they failed to obtain control over the countryside, the British learned that the "forward policy" was self-defeating. They returned to the formula of subsidizing the Afghan government in return for control over its foreign affairs. Events had also shown that Anglo-Russian concerns elsewhere outbalanced whatever gains either side might win from interference in Afghanistan. Beginning in the 1880's the two powers agreed to cooperate, the Afghan-Russian boundaries were defined, British supervision of Afghan diplomacy was acknowledged, and later a modest amount of trade across the Amu Darya was allowed to develop.

The consequences for Afghanistan of these rivalries and wars were serious and enduring. The political system had to be completely reconstructed after each of the invasions. The fact that tribal forces had mounted the only effective opposition to the British made these tasks even more difficult. In winning political control the amirs had to make concessions to the tribes. At best, therefore, the wars had made unification exceedingly difficult.

It was obvious to the amirs that they had to depend upon the British for the military and economic support necessary to begin the building of effective government. Thus, they were forced to cooperate with the very force which had badly damaged their political prospects. Inevitably, hate and distrust of the British came to be mixed with dependence upon them. These attitudes affected Afghan understanding of innovations in European science, thought, and government. On the one hand it was often possible for the amirs to rail against British influence and manipulate hatred of the British in order to rally opposing internal forces to their cause. But the need to use military and technical improvements to ensure royal control demanded an almost schizophrenic posture of reliance upon the British as the main source of innovation. This posture tended to limit Afghan interests in modern technology to military logistics and the production of war equipment. The attitude of Afghanistan's political leadership until the end of the nineteenth century thus supported an extremely selective modernization. The amirs were determined that the kingdom's cultural and social life would not be affected by it.

Until 1880 internal divisions and external intrusions had prevented the establishment of an effective central government. Several minority communities, especially some of the Turks and the Hazaras, retained their independence, while the powerful Pushtun tribes expected to dictate the fate of the government. Little permanent progress in establishing a state had been made in more than 130 years of effort. The swelling tides of European power and ambition made the prospects for the separate existence of Afghanistan increasingly dim. Yet, even with these bleak circumstances, a new amir was able to subdue all internal resistance to centralized political authority, and his successors were able to win European acceptance of Afghan independence.

Centralization, Modernization, and Independence, 1880–1929

AMIR ABDUR RAHMAN, 1880–1901

Abdur Rahman agreed in 1880 to British supervision over foreign affairs in return for a subsidy and noninterference in his attempts to gain control over the entire country. Shortly thereafter he was able to defeat his rivals in Kandahar and Herat and achieve nominal unification.

The amir developed a doctrine of royal authority which rejected tribal election as too restrictive of his powers. He claimed that he ruled by divine right, not as the leader of a confederacy of Durrani tribes. This argument asserted that the sovereignty residing in the Afghan people was a creation of God and the authority of the ruler whom they elected was, therefore, sacred. It enabled him to combine the sentiment of nationality with resentment against the British. Afghan Islam could be protected from further Christian influences only by a strong, unified government. And because his authority had divine origin and its usage was ultimately religious, he claimed that his power must be total. Opposition, either political or religious, constituted treason both to the state and to Islam. On this basis the amir could argue that steps to modernize government, especially to increase royal military strength, were consistent with the perpetuation of internal cultural and religious traditions. This doctrine won results largely because of the will, intelligence, and political skill of the amir, but its price was the inauguration of a conservative-modernist conflict within Afghan leadership.

Abdur Rahman courted public opinion through policies which dramatized the religious justification for his authority. He conquered the Hazaras, who are mostly Shiites, and took credit for having imposed the dominance of the Sunni majority over a religious minority. This strategy was carried further in the 1890's when he declared holy war against the pagan Kafirs of eastern Afghanistan. Their conquest and subsequent conversion to Islam (and the change of their name to Nuristanis—people of the land of light) gained for the amir the title of religious deliverer.

Abdur Rahman reinforced these doctrinal claims and popular gestures with a variety of practical methods, some of them brutally repressive, to ensure a monopoly of power. He strengthened the army by improving its organization, training, and logistical capabilities. Its loyalty and morale were also improved by regular payment of salaries raised for the first time to levels which met subsistence needs. Military recruitment was based upon universal conscription. Increases were also made in the government's capacity to manufacture its own military equipment: small arms, field artillery, and numerous noncombat items. Nonmilitary production also was attempted partly to make the royal household, as well as the army, less dependent on foreign suppliers. Modern methods of manufacturing leather goods, glass, furniture, textiles, and clothing were first carried out in these military facilities.

Such technological innovations were essential to the amir's pretensions to absolute power. However, they depended upon the administrative apparatus which raised the revenue to pay for them. Expansion and rationalization of administration was the first requirement for royal authority. The steps which Abdur Rahman took laid the foundation for the modern structure of the Afghan state. An attempt was made to organize the government into functional departments. The organization of records and the clerical staff needed to prepare and use them were given high priority. But progress was limited; few Afghans had appropriate education and many of those who were qualified were not willing to work in a government in which suspicion of dishonesty—often warranted—could lead to the loss of a hand or summary execution. Nevertheless, an organized bureaucracy slowly began to emerge.

The administrative apparatus was extended to provincial and subprovincial levels. Provinces were established in regions dominated by the four major cities of Kabul, Kandahar, Herat, and Mazar-i-Sharif. The main functions of these subordinate governments were the maintenance of order, assurance of justice, assessment and collection of taxes, and application of the military conscription law. Little is known as yet about the effectiveness of provincial government under Abdur Rahman. The presence of central authority was obviously demonstrated. Tax collection and the reliability of the records upon which it was based notably improved. Even so, the amir himself stated that only one quarter of the taxes were paid willingly, one quarter had to be fought for, one quarter were lost, and the population was ignorant of where and to which authority to pay the remaining quarter.

Abdur Rahman also tightened control over the religious establishment. In addition to declaring himself to be the religious head of Afghanistan, he incorporated the Muslim clergy into government service. The mullahs in the villages and the Muslim judges of various ranks were made dependent upon the government for promotion, income, and to some extent for prestige. Expropriation of religious property was also used to end ecclesiastical autonomy. The amir moved also to abolish the virtual independence exercised by the clergy in interpreting and enforcing law. Court decisions were made subject to review by secular officials. Crimes against the state were reserved for royal jurisdiction. Thus, while Afghanistan's religious leaders continued to play major social and legal roles, the government asserted ultimate control over them.

Abdur Rahman's contribution to modernization was concentrated in increasing the ruling capacity of the central government, although he did attempt to introduce some modest improvements in trade, roads, and the legal position of women. For the most part, however, he had a modern outlook only in matters of political power. With the important exception of the establishment of peace throughout the country, Afghans received few direct benefits during his reign. Nevertheless, an apparatus had been built that his successors could use to widen the diffusion of services and opportunities possible with effective operation of a modern government.

Extremely tough in his internal policies, the amir was

nimble and conciliatory in his conduct of external affairs. He recognized that in order to have a free hand to consolidate his authority at home he had to ensure that both the British and the Russians would accept his regime. To that end he accepted British tutelage in foreign affairs, which meant that he was denied direct foreign relations with any other power, including the Russians. He demonstrated his willingness to cooperate with British efforts to pacify the Pushtun tribes along the eastern frontier by relinquishing Afghan jurisdiction over the land and people east of the Durand Line in 1893. This was a fateful concession; it divided several tribes virtually in half, and it subjected Abdur Rahman and the monarchs who have come after him to internal pressures to reopen the issue. A realist, though, the amir saw that he was ceding authority over tribes whom he himself could not control, in return for a renewed British guarantee of political support and an increased subsidy with which to build his army. In the last years of his reign, Abdur Rahman resented the aggressive tactics which the British used against the tribes, but he put the perfection of his power ahead of pretensions to rule all Pushtuns.

PROGRESS AND CONTINUITY UNDER HABIBULLAH, 1901–1919

Afghanistan experienced one of its smoothest successions when Habibullah ascended the throne in 1901. He was well trained and sufficiently mature to build upon the accomplishments of his father. He retained the latter's twin goals of preventing foreign intervention and maintaining the royal grip on internal power, but to a considerable degree he was able to soften the methods which Abdur Rahman had used to eliminate opposition. Honors and appointments were frequently used as devices to win the support of tribal and religious leaders.

Another departure was Habibullah's commitment to wider modernization. During his reign the trickle of foreign technical, ideological, and aesthetic influences widened into a stream. It was becoming increasingly difficult for Afghans to ignore the economic and ideological as well as the political implications of the global changes taking place in the years before World War I.

Concerned that many aspects of modernization would meet great hostility from conservatives, Habibullah stressed that a strong government could shield Islamic institutions and that further military and economic innovations were necessary for this strength. He complemented this argument with an adroit diplomacy which won continued British support while frustrating British demands for military and economic concessions. More popular was Habibullah's encouragement of the Muslim states, especially Turkey, in their struggles with the Christian powers of Europe. Pan-Islamism was an issue that could unite the radical conservatives and modernists among his subjects.

With Habibullah's support a modernist and nationalist elite developed for the first time in Afghanistan. This small group advocated sweeping social, cultural, and economic changes. Not surprisingly, it did not advocate political change; its members argued instead that Habibullah's benevolent despotism was the appropriate instrument of reform.

The greatest progress was made in education, journalism, and technology. No systematic educational measures had been undertaken by Abdur Rahman. The field was fraught with potential traditionalist opposition. Modern education would invariably bring western science and sociopolitical ideas into the schools. Such steps were directly opposed to the mullahs' insistence that education was primarily for learning the precepts and theology of Islam. The modernists argued that such alien teachings ultimately would enable Afghanistan to survive as an Islamic society. Each new educational experiment was conducted discreetly. Only a small number of royal family members, their relatives, and close retainers was allowed access to the training established at the new military college and at Habibiya, the nation's first modern secondary school. The risk of opposition was further minimized by a gradual introduction of new subjects. Habibiya's curriculum remained predominantly traditional for more than ten years after its founding in 1904. Direct European influence was kept to a minimum; Turks and Muslim Indians were employed as teachers.

Habibullah also founded several professional and vocational schools in the fields of administration, arts and crafts, and teacher training. Such innovations were to produce the first crop of leaders whose ideas and goals were influenced by norms outside of traditional patterns. From the 1920's onward, these limited educational beginnings were to have increasing impact upon the evolution of government.

Modern journalism was inaugurated, although it was confined to an elite, urban audience by a literacy rate which was probably lower than 2 per cent. Despite this limitation, journals controlled and financed by government infused new ideas and vitality into the political system.

The most influential of early Afghan journalists was Mahmud Tarzi, a Durrani nobleman whose family had been exiled by Abdur Rahman. His education at Damascus and Istanbul prepared Tarzi for the role of spokesman for modernism, nationalism, and Pan-Islamism. He founded Afghanistan's first newspaper, *Siraj-al-Akhbar* (The Lamp of News), in 1911. As editor, he contributed articles devoted to technology, education, contemporary affairs, and social comment. Habibullah used him and like-minded intellectuals to test Afghan receptivity to innovations without having to associate himself directly.

Before World War I, an increasingly ambitious range of technical innovations was attempted. A small hydroelectric plant was built near Kabul. The road system was extended. New facilities were added to the military workshops. Nevertheless, modern changes under Habibullah affected Afghan society only superficially. To some extent this was due to his sensitivity to the threat of foreign domination. With considerable skill he prevented British or Russian activities within the country except on his own terms.

Formerly accepted views of the realities of international politics were sorely tested by World War I. The Europeans demonstrated to the Afghans and other non-Western peoples that Western culture was capable of self-destruction. Afghan modernists were confronted with the realization that Europe did not have all the answers to the needs of modern society. On the other hand, the Islamic community had also behaved disappointingly. The Arab revolt against the Turkish Empire and the general willingness of Muslims throughout the world to ally with non-Muslim powers were disillusioning and disconcerting.

Aside from these changes in the general direction of international affairs, the war affected Afghanistan directly. Its most powerful neighbors emerged greatly changed. The revolutions and civil war in Russia had opened up possibilities for new relationships with Afghanistan. From Czarist imperialism, Russian foreign policy under Lenin apparently swung full circle to support of "anti-imperialist" struggles of Asian peoples against European domination. In addition, the fate of the Muslim population in Russian Turkistan was to remain uncertain for several years. This situation provided an opportunity for greater Afghan influence in the region, even though such ambitions conflicted with the intentions of the new Bolshevik regime.

While less spectacular, changes created in the political landscape of British India were almost as fundamental. In 1919 the government of India faced a militant nationalist movement most of whose factions would shortly demand independence. The British no longer held a secure base from which they could enforce their will upon the Pushtun tribes or interfere in Afghan affairs. A new era in Afghanistan's foreign relations had suddenly become possible.

AMANULLAH: INDEPENDENCE, REFORM, AND CATASTROPHE

For Afghanistan these external changes were combined with the danger of chaos following the assassination of Habibullah in January, 1919. His death unleashed a struggle for the throne which was quickly won by his third son, Amanullah. In making good his claim, Amanullah had to react to a rapidly changing course of international and internal events. He became convinced that

Indian unrest gave him an opportunity both to solidify his internal support and to win complete independence from the British. Two months after seizing power, he sent the Afghan army against British positions east of the Durand Line. After a sharp series of engagements, a cease fire led to an agreement by which the British gave up all supervisory claims and the amir lost his subsidy. This short war is known in Afghanistan as the Third War of Independence.

Relations with Russia also broke new ground. Friendly Bolshevik overtures and Amanullah's desire to find a diplomatic counterweight to the British led to the Russo-Afghan Friendship Treaty of 1919. In addition to mutual guarantees of friendship and nonbelligerence, the Russians undertook to provide technical and economic assistance. For the first time formal and apparently enthusiastic relations were established between the two governments. There remained, however, the question of the future of the Muslim population north of the Amu Darya where anticommunist governments had been organized. This situation offered Afghans the opportunity to champion the independence of brother Muslims. In 1920 and 1921 Amanullah and the Russians played a double game of ostensible friendship while contending for control over Turkistan. The rivalry ended with a major Bolshevik victory. As a result many Turkomans who had fought the communists, sought and won asylum in Afghanistan.

Following these aggressive thrusts during his first two years as king, Amanullah adopted a policy of cooperation with his two major neighbors. He was willing to normalize relations in order to concentrate upon his plans for domestic reform. But one major novelty was added to foreign policy. To offset dependence upon either the Russians or the British, Amanullah sought aid from other European powers and the newly emerging Muslim states of the Middle East. He cultivated close relations with France, Germany, Italy, the Republic of Turkey, and Iran. The long-standing policy of isolation was ended.

Amanullah had become king with a modernist reputation. Unlike his father and grandfather, he did not assert religious sanctions as part of the foundation for royal authority. His own view of the legitimacy of his position as ruler appears to have been totally nationalist. For a time the achievement of independence strengthened this claim. However, his secularist views and actions rankled conservative religious leaders more deeply than had Abdur Rahman's seizure of their offices and property. His breaks with the past in his attempts to put modernization into practice constitute a major chapter in the evolution of contemporary Afghan society. While his programs were often continuations of earlier efforts, his style of leadership was new. He envisioned modernization primarily as educational, social, and cultural change. He emphasized new attitudes, ideas, knowledge, and styles of behavior. Modernization was seen more as a problem of persuasion than as a process of institution building.

Education was the field of most ambitious reforms. One goal was a national system of schools with a modern curriculum. The beginnings of a network of government-run intermediate and secondary schools was achieved in 1928; as many as 40,000 students were enrolled. Vocational and professional training, especially for teachers, was greatly expanded.

Amanullah introduced two important educational innovations: higher education programs in France, Germany, and Italy for children of leading Afghan families, and the establishment of officially supported education for women. An intermediate school for girls was founded in Kabul with the sponsorship of the queen in 1924.

Educational change was accompanied by pressure to loosen restrictions upon women's roles in society. Laws were passed which gave women virtually equal rights in marriage and divorce, and equal inheritance rights with their brothers and sons. The authority of the Shariah and of the tribal codes was eroded by laws and ordinances which attempted to humanize criminal punishments and to restrict the authority of the Muslim jurists. Thus, Amanullah diminished the influence of religious conservatives in the fields of both education and justice.

His era also witnessed the rapid expansion of journalism. Several provincial newspapers were published, in addition to official daily and weekly publications in Kabul, all of which attempted to argue for acceptance of the government-sponsored reforms.

These often provocative changes were not accompanied by effective efforts to improve the army or the government bureaucracy. Some new forms of military equipment, most notably airplanes and radios, were introduced, but Amanullah's policies and the administrative weaknesses of the government kept army morale and efficiency dangerously low. As a consequence it became an uncertain source of support against the accumulating resentment among the traditionalists in the tribes and the mosques.

Amanullah had no coherent plan to encourage economic improvements. Little was done to expand foreign trade or to introduce industrial facilities. Lacking a rising national income, he was forced to finance his educational schemes by increasing the taxes on commerce and agriculture, thus aggravating the hostility to the reforms.

In 1927, after eight years of effort, few of Amanullah's reforms had gotten beyond planning or elementary stages. At this point he embarked on an unprecedented tour of Western Asia and Europe. Between late 1927 and mid-1928 the king visited India, Iran, Turkey, Egypt, Italy, France, England, Germany, the Soviet Union, and several smaller nations. The tour gave him first-hand impressions of modern economic and political systems. Much attention was given to observing technical achievements, and to extending Afghan diplomatic connections throughout Europe.

It was an enormously exciting experience. Amanullah returned home convinced that the pace of modernization had to be quickened. His impatience with Afghan reluctance to accept new forms of government, economic activity, innovative ideas, or new styles of life grew to the point where he no longer accepted counsels of caution on the pace of change. He convened a national meeting of all tribal leaders (a Loya Jirga) to which he outlined a program far more ambitious than his earlier schemes. The government was to become a democratic, parliamentary monarchy. The army was to be greatly enlarged through the imposition of a compulsory draft, and was to be financed by a 10 per cent reduction in the pay of all civil officials. Immediate construction of a national system of railways was to begin. No time was to be lost also in establishing free universal education, not only for boys, but for girls between the ages of six and eleven. All noble titles were to be eliminated.

These demands incensed Afghan conservatives. It was obvious that most of them were unenforceable. There were no resources to make more than the smallest beginnings in military, educational, or construction projects. Far more distressing to many influential Afghans were Amanullah's pronouncements on marriage, the social role of women, and insistence upon Western dress. The king asked the jirga to outlaw any form of polygamy, despite its sanction in Islamic law. Moreover, it was to be lawful for women to discard the chaudury (the traditional garment which covered both head and body). More bizarre was Amanullah's order that all persons in Kabul must wear Western-style clothes. This applied to rural visitors and led to a brisk business in clothing rentals at the outskirts of the city.

Amanullah's sincerity as a patriot did little to offset the outrage of his military and civil officials, as well as the religious and tribal leadership. Within weeks of the announcement of these new policies rebellions began among the Pushtun tribes. Civil authority broke down even among the normally peaceful Tajiks. By the end of 1928 the government was near collapse. Bandits gained control of the countryside and one band laid siege to Kabul itself. When army units refused to defend the city, Amanullah abdicated; his unpopularity threatened total destruction of the government. After a brief attempt to rally support at Kandahar, he left Afghanistan for exile in Italy where he died in 1960.

Kabul was seized by an outlaw peasant, Bacha-i-Sachao, who attempted to win support by abolishing most of Amanullah's reforms, moderate and radical. Commerce again stagnated and the national army dissolved leaving the country divided between rule by bandit gangs and the tribal khans.

Despite support from religious leaders and toleration from some khans who preferred a weak central government which could not interfere in their affairs, Bacha-i-Sachao had little opportunity to consolidate power. A Tajik, he threatened the end of Pushtun rule. In order to pay his own troops he had to resort to the plundering of whatever private wealth he could find. Merchants naturally turned against the new regime and eventually offered financial help to rival pretenders.

Both the British and the Russian governments were alarmed at the chaos that was spreading under the rebels in Afghanistan. The Soviets had invested ten years of support in Amanullah and, despite the fact that Bacha came from a class that was certainly low enough to be suitably revolutionary, they labeled his rebellion as feudal and reactionary. They blamed Amanullah's fall on British intrigue. For their part the British were worried that the collapse of Afghan government threatened their control over the tribes along the frontier. Even more disconcerting was the possibility that the Russians would take advantage of the political vacuum. Thus, both powerful neighbors withheld recognition and support from the rebel regime.

Opposition within and outside Afghanistan crystallized under the leadership of Nadir Khan in the spring of 1929. He was the leader of the Musahiban family which was descended from the royal Sadozai and Mohammedzai clans and therefore was an eligible claimant to the throne in the view of other Pushtuns. His reputation as a patriot was well established. As commander in chief he had led

Afghan units in their most successful engagements against the British in the 1919 war. Having disagreed with Amanullah, partially over questions of reform, Nadir had retired to France in the mid-1920's.

After several abortive campaigns Nadir Khan captured Kabul in October, 1929. Apparently at the insistence of his own followers, he then accepted the title of shah or king; thus canceling Amanullah's claim. The dynasty Nadir Shah founded is the one which still reigns under his son, Zahir Shah.

Musahiban Rule, 1929–1963

With the restoration of Durrani rule, Afghanistan began a slow recovery from its devastating political collapse. Modernization had been reversed; its advocates either killed or exiled. The experience suggested that great caution was required in the installation of social or even technical changes. Nadir Shah recognized that his regime had first to establish political and military power, which required the allegiance of conservative secular and religious leaders, before efforts to induce further changes could be seriously entertained. Thus he concentrated his efforts on the rebuilding of government authority.

Ratification of his right to rule was given by a new Loya Jirga in 1931, which accepted a new constitution establishing Nadir's family as the reigning dynasty. The constitution resurrected royal absolutism and re-created an advisory parliament. Actual setting and execution of policy became a practical monopoly of the king and his four brothers. Afghanistan was to be governed essentially by a family oligarchy.

The new regime stressed Islamic traditions and laws as

the basis for its authority, discarding Amanullah's secularist, nationalist theory of legitimacy. Concessions were
made to religious conservatives in the fields of women's
rights and Islamic law. When the kingdom's one girl's
school was reopened, it was to train nurses, not to provide
a general, modern education. The government relaxed its
claim of control over school curricula, and Muslim judges
were given more latitude to interpret law than they had
had since before the reign of Abdur Rahman. It was not to
be until 1959 that the new dynasty was confident enough of
its authority to support the unveiling of women. Prior to
that time, however, cautious steps were undertaken to
modernize the educational and judicial systems.

Nadir Shah and his brothers moved to initiate substantial economic development. The first step was taken in
1932 with the establishment of the kingdom's first modern
economic organization, the Bank-i-Milli (national bank).
It was to hold both government and private deposits.
These funds were used to develop foreign trade and to
set up industrial operations within the country. It was
expected to channel profits from expanding foreign trade
into investments which could modernize the internal
economy. Although the government retained supervisory
control, the Bank-i-Milli made possible unprecedented
opportunities for private profit. It financed private firms
to which the government gave monopoly licenses for the
most lucrative segments of Afghanistan's export and import trade. Growing imports of petroleum, textiles,
vehicles, machinery, and luxury goods were handled by
these firms. Considerable development of primary export
products was also achieved, particularly in karakul skins,
wool, and fruit. As the volume of trade grew, the govern-

ment was able to extract a growing share of revenue which it used to build its civil and military administration and for improved communications and transportation.

A modest industrial foundation was laid. Textile mills and cement plants were started and government workshop operations were further enlarged. For the first time since the First World War, the country's hydroelectric capacity was expanded.

Nadir Shah's attempts to restore royal authority were cut short by his assassination in 1933. The tragedy illustrated the continuing influence of tribal mores within the political system. The king was killed by a cadet at the royal military school whose patron had been summarily executed for treason by Nadir Shah. The execution had not only been an affair of state; it had also resulted from a blood feud between the royal family and another prominent Mohammedzai family.

The Musahiban regime continued under the leadership of Nadir Shah's three surviving brothers, Mohammed Hashim Khan, Shah Mahmud, and Wali Shah. They ran the government jointly after having placed Nadir Shah's oldest son, Zahir, then a youth of nineteen, on the throne. Over the next thirteen years Mohammed Hashim Khan was prime minister in the family-run government. He continued the policy of combining gradual innovation with the building of the central government's military and civil power. The most notable progress came in the economy. The amount of capital generated by the investments of the Bank-i-Milli multiplied as much as one hundred times in the 1930's, and the volume of foreign trade increased greatly. Significant results had been achieved in domestic sugar refining, and cotton and wool textile, soap, and leather manufacturing by the beginning of the Second World War. However, conflicts arose within the economic program. Profits from expanded foreign trade were much greater than could be generated by the new manufacturing operations. Moreover, the policy of encouraging manufactured imports weakened investor interests in establishing factories which might compete with them. Recognition of these problems, and a desire to control the size of some spectacularly rising private fortunes, led to the decision to remove the government's own deposits from the Bank-i-Milli in 1939. They were placed in a totally government-controlled institution, the Da Afghanistan Bank.

A significant result of economic growth in the 1930's was the rise of political influence based upon commercial wealth. Ethnically divided between the Uzbek, Indian, and Tajik minorities, merchant influence in the past had been regional or local in scope. With the organization of nationwide capital and credit mechanisms it was now possible for the most aggressive and knowledgeable merchants to gain control over large sectors of the expanding foreign and internal trade.

German assistance became increasingly prominent in Afghan development during the 1930's. Industrial and power facilities and the construction of schools and government buildings were in large part made possible by German technical advice and credits. Japanese, East European, and French aid was also important.

By 1935 the regime felt confident enough to embark upon new attempts to develop education. A fresh objective was added: Pushtun dominance was to be equated with national and cultural unity. The development of Pushtu as the language of government and education was encouraged at the expense of Persian. Fluency and literacy in Pushtu were required in the upper school grades and expected of middle and senior level government officials. The Pushtun Academy and the Afghan Historical Society were founded for the purposes of sponsoring research which was intended to reinforce a sense of common nationality among the Pushtuns and the minority groups.

The effort to stimulate patriotism was closely related to the expansion of the school system. The skills, knowledge, and attitudes required for modernization were reinstated as another major goal of education. Considerable over-all progress was made in increasing the numbers of teachers and students. By 1946 there were nearly 3,000 teachers and 100,000 students in government schools. This represented only a beginning, however, since less than 10 per cent of school-age children had access to school and 80 per cent of the educational facilities were confined to Kabul.

Other elements necessary for the full development of education were introduced during this era. Higher education in Afghanistan began in 1932 with the establishment of a medical college aided by a French mission. By the middle of World War II, colleges had also been developed in political science and law, theology, and letters. The Ministry of Education began the difficult task of preparing and publishing textbooks. In almost every respect the educational apparatus remained primitive, but the government's commitment to improving and extending it was underscored by its priority in the national budget where it held second place behind military expenditures.

The strength of the national army relative to the power of the tribes remained crucial for the authority of the government. The Musahibans moved cautiously toward the long-sought goal of an effective centrally controlled system of military conscription. The international dangers of the 1940's finally made this possible. Threats to Afghan neutrality during World War II gave the government an opportunity to win tribal compliance with a draft system. This achievement and the gradual strengthening of its fighting and technical capacities soon were to make the royal army superior to any potential internal opposition.

Efforts to support modest development programs through a policy of international neutrality ran into increasing difficulties as war in Europe again approached. The prominance of the Italian and German missions annoyed the British and the Russians. The British in particular feared intrigue among the frontier tribes. Afghan acceptance of assistance was interpreted as a device for German, Italian, and Japanese control over segments of the economy. Consequently, a diplomatic crisis occurred after the war began. Several hundred citizens of the Axis powers were stranded in Afghanistan. Much of the supplies and financing for roads, dams, radio communications, and light industrial plants upon which they were working were cut off. After becoming allies in 1941, the British and Russians insisted that these foreigners be interned or expelled. The Afghans had no choice but to comply.

This intrusion into Afghan internal affairs and wartime conditions generally inflicted severe damage on the economy. The fledgling modern sectors were badly disrupted. Progress made earlier in internationalizing and commercializing agriculture meant that the loss of markets and of access to imports and credits hurt the economy far more seriously than could have happened prior to the beginnings of development. Inflation, especially ruinous to urban workingmen and government employees, more than tripled prices during the war. Disruptions to the economy cost heavily in development delays and illustrated how vulnerable Afghanistan remained to outside forces.

The combination of political and economic problems which followed World War II led to a political change. In 1946, Shah Mahmud replaced his older brother, Mohammed Hashim, as prime minister. During his seven years of rule, attempts were made to solve the political and economic problems brought into prominence in the course of the war. A tiny, but outspoken group of intellectuals called for the relaxation of autocratic rule. Shah Mahmud moved to mollify them and to resume economic development. Foreign relations came to be dominated by a dispute with Pakistan over Pushtunistan, the official Afghan term for the Pushtun areas east of the Durand Line. This issue created hostility between the two Muslim governments immediately upon the founding of Pakistan in August, 1947. For Afghanistan it was to have serious domestic as well as international consequences.

Efforts in the late 1940's and early 1950's to bring about economic improvements while finding a means to channel political opposition toward support for the government proved to be difficult. Heavy reliance was placed upon American help with an ambitious project to develop the Helmand Valley region. When the project bogged down in the early 1950's, the government's entire economic development program came under fire from Afghan critics, who, in the meantime had been permitted to organize political parties and private journals. Between 1949 and 1952, Shah Mahmud allowed the parliament created by the 1931 Constitution to be dominated by a group of some fifty reform members. Official alarm arose when public criticism of the government broadened to include demands for removal of the cabinet and even the king. Antigovernment agitation involved students from Kabul University. By 1952, the government was faced with growing dissent which threatened disruption of its own operations and the radicalization of the kingdom's only center for higher learning. These discouragements, combined with slow economic progress and the failure to gain satisfaction on the Pushtunistan issue, brought about the cabinet's resignation in 1953 and Shah Mahmud's replacement by Prince Daud, his nephew and a first cousin to the king.

Concluding that Afghanistan could not simultaneously develop politically and economically, Daud unambiguously chose economic growth. Parliament was ignored, private publications were banned, and some outspoken critics were jailed, although a few of these were later released to serve in important positions within the government itself. It was under Daud's direction that the decision was made to accept Russian and East European economic and military aid, as discussed in Chapter 4.

Despite the continuation of royal oligarchy, progress was made in the professionalism of administration. Ministries in the development fields were either founded or reorganized, and a group of civil servants, selected largely on the basis of foreign technical or professional training, filled high offices. Under Daud this small corps of capable officials accumulated valuable development experience.

Pushtunistan was the prime minister's other major concern. Considerable pressure for an adamant position appears to have been exerted upon the government by some of the tribes living on the Afghan side of the eastern frontier. As put forward in 1947, the Afghan position was that the population of Pushtunistan—usually described as the area lying east of the Durand Line, but in some statements as all of West Pakistan west of the Indus River—should have the option, through a plebiscite, to decide for independence or for inclusion within India or Pakistan. Most estimates place roughly one-half of the total Pushtun population east of the Durand Line making it appear likely that the Afghan government would have interpreted independence for Pushtunistan to mean close political association with Afghanistan. Such a result would have, in effect, restored Afghan access to the Peshawar region and perhaps even to the Arabian Sea.

Using the garrison and loose administrative system inherited from the British, Pakistan retained its hold over the disputed tribal region. Resistance to Pakistani control, encouraged and on occasion overtly supported by the Afghan government, produced a series of crises, especially in the mid-1950's and early 1960's. The incorporation of all West Pakistan, including the Pushtun area, into one administrative unit in 1955 was seen by Afghans as an attempt to destroy the cultural and political uniqueness of the tribal region. In 1961 skirmishes between detachments of the two national armies brought about the closing of the border to trade and nomadic migrations.

Afghanistan suffered from serious disadvantages in attempting to exert pressure on Pakistan. By controlling the region in question, Pakistan also controlled trade connections which were essential to Afghanistan. Denied access to the territory itself and unlikely to win a full-scale war, the Afghans turned to the two devices available to them: support for the "Free Pushtunistan" underground, and the recruitment of allies. Neither proved sufficient to loosen Pakistan's grip. The Pushtun inclination to remain free of outside control was successfully neutralized by the introduction of economic opportunities and provision for considerable tribal autonomy. The Russians were Afghanistan's major success in the search for allies on the issue, but Soviet support was partially counterbalanced by the awkward policy of the United States which supplied arms to Pakistan and accepted the Pakistani argument that the Durand Line was an international frontier, while trying simultaneously to remain on friendly terms with Afghanistan.

During the later years of the Daud regime, the disruption of trade through Peshawar and Quetta caused by the dispute created serious delays in deliveries of American and West European assistance supplies. It also denied Afghanistan direct access to Pakistan for the sale of fresh produce, a major source of foreign currency. With Russian help, an airlift to India salvaged a large part of the annual fruit exports in 1961 and 1962, but the episode demonstrated the price that Afghanistan was paying in loss of economic opportunities and international freedom of action.

Prince Daud resolutely steered Afghanistan through a period of serious internal pressures and sharp turns in foreign policy. In the early 1960's, demands again built up within the expanding educated elite for a broader system of political participation. His considerable accomplishments—the harnessing of vast amounts of foreign aid, the elimination of tribal threats to the government through modernization of the army, the further expansion of modern forms of education, and the effective deveiling of women—were seen as laying the foundations for a new set of policies. The view that progress under such leadership had achieved as much as was possible, coupled with the liabilities accumulating from Daud's intransigent position on Pushtunistan, paved the way for a new government as well as a new era in 1963.

3. Government:
Structure and Functions

Central authority has slowly and painfully been able to spread in Afghanistan during the twentieth century despite the persistence of tribal, regional, and ethnic loyalties. In the 1960's this authoritarian trend was softened by a genuine attempt to introduce constitutionalism, but survival of the government continues to require a tight grip on the traditional sources of power. The setback suffered by the monarchy in 1929 serves as a reminder that control and stability cannot be taken for granted.

The present structure of the Afghan state is the creation of the dynasty of Nadir Shah, although much of the precedent and strategy for nation-building extends back even to Dost Mohammed. Faced with the task of building a government from virtually nothing, the Musahiban family has created effective rule by welding together several elements essential to political power. These include: the royal family itself, the military forces, private economic interests, especially large landowners and commercial capitalists, the religious leadership, surviving tribal authority, and the rapidly growing Western-educated professional class which staffs the government ministries and private firms. Altogether, these leadership elements comprise a small percentage of the total population. They do not include the middle or lower class of junior officials, shopkeepers, and landowning peasants who as yet have little influence.

While the narrowness of the community which holds power may suggest that privileged oligarchy has replaced egalitarian social traditions, recent government policy has made clear the intention to broaden the sharing of political power. This delegation of power involves considerable risk to the royal family and its allies. While the effort is buttressed to some extent by the democratic vestiges and autonomous traditions which survive in Afghan institutions, modern state-building has required bureaucratic autocracy and the establishment of control from above over the clan, tribe, and village. Consequently, the pace of decentralization has been controlled by the oligarchy allied with the throne. Whether this leadership can maintain control as the process accelerates is the most crucial question for Afghanistan's future.

The Royal Family

The reigning family is from the Yahya Khel lineage of the Mohammedzai clan of the Barakzai branch of the Durrani tribe. Its claim to legitimacy is partially based upon inheritance, which is essential but not sufficient to ensure acquiescence to its authority. The threat of rivalry between royal clans remains latent. Musahiban achievements in pacifying, unifying, and partially modernizing the country form the most persuasive basis for the dynasty's support. This success has altered the requirements for continued rule. The royal family has had to respond to the political changes for which it itself has been responsible.

Its policies have been an amalgam of the traditional and the modern. Many of the more powerful Pushtun tribes have direct links with the monarchy based upon reciprocal obligations from past services. Tradition also establishes an important connection between the secular ruler and Islam. New elements have added to the pre-eminence of the royal family over the past two generations: its internal unity, the effectiveness of its own members in major government offices, and its policy of mollifying other powerful Durrani families with lesser honors and posts to ensure their loyalty. Following the personal leadership provided by his father, his uncles, and his cousin, Zahir Shah has increasingly demonstrated political craftsmanship. It is probably more than coincidence that each of the kings and prime ministers furnished by this family have lived and studied abroad. No previous dynasty had access to a modern education. These personal qualities and the record of accomplishment, combined with inherited sources of allegiance, have enabled the dynasty to bring together the forces essential for governing Afghanistan during an era of rapid transition from traditional to modern political institutions.

Military Forces

The growth of royal power is intimately related to the establishment of modern forms of military organization under centralized control. Having been installed on the throne by a temporary alliance of the southern tribes in 1929, Musahiban authority could not become permanent without a reliable professional army with modern training, organization, and equipment. Largely on the basis of Russian assistance in recent years, a national force has been developed which has greatly strengthened the hand of the government.

The army is the most modern institution in the nation. Its officers are the product of foreign and scientific education, and its enlisted men are themselves an elite group with respect to technical training. These accomplishments have been costly. The military budget takes a high proportion of total government expenditure (its exact amount is not made public). Even more burdensome is Afghanistan's dependence on foreign help to maintain the military forces at their present level of sophistication. The employment of MG-17's, tanks, radio communications, heavy artillery, and the logistical means to support such equipment are beyond the capacity of Afghan society to pay for, equip, or train. Consequently, the government has exchanged its vulnerability to the potential internal menace of tribal rebellion for the possible external threat of Russian intervention.

While it has not been possible for the government to control effectively the new sources of its military power, the vast increase in its military strength is unquestioned. So long as the components of the officer corps retain the loyalty which they have so far shown to the king, the military establishment will continue to be the most potent element of state power. The army and air force are kept insulated from politics generally. Little is publicly known of the political attitudes of the officers and men. While there is much speculation on the political role of the military, especially in view of the prominent part in politics being played by soldiers in several of Afghanistan's neighbors, even during the unrest and uncertainty which have attended the implementation of the 1964

Constitution, there has been no sign of the military becoming an autonomous political force.

Major Landed and Commercial Interests

The processes of government centralization and economic modernization have permitted a few landowning
and commercial families to become wealthy beyond any
Afghan precedent. To some extent contemporary large
landholding has been related to expansion of Pushtun,
largely Durrani, control over agricultural areas that were
earlier held by other ethnic groups. However, the emergence of large landlords as a class cuts across ethnic lines
and, for the most part, it is limited to some of the most
prosperous valley regions.

Much more notable has been the rapid increase in
wealth achieved by investors and managers of firms en-
gaged in modern forms of production, import-export
trading, and banking. Multimillion dollar personal fortunes have been amassed. The skill, experience, foreign
contacts, and capital resources of this small group of entrepreneurs are assets in the efforts of the government to
expand economic development. The friction begun in the
1930's between the government and private capitalists has
persisted, however. Public-private rivalry continues despite the prominent roles which individual Afghan businessmen have recently played in the development of
official financial and industrial agencies. Mutuality of
interests has insured cooperation, and private capital is
depended upon for a major share of investment inputs in
the most recent stages of economic planning. The government controls private investment, but it has conceded,
ruefully at times, that toleration of a high-profit sector is,

at least temporarily, in the interests of economic growth and political stability. Private capital is one of the more visible issues in Afghan politics. It has become the target of increasing criticism from a few intellectuals and politicians who wish to see complete or nearly complete public control over the modern sectors of the economy.

Religious Leadership

The present dynasty has achieved a large share of its stability from having successfully incorporated religious specialists into government service and by emphasizing the religious components of its authority. The regime has set out to enlist the clergy's support in the process of state-building and, profiting from Amanullah's example, it has succeeded to a large degree. Religious authority is still primarily based upon the personal behavior of the village mullah, and his hostility toward the growing power and secularization of the central government appears to have softened. To some extent this has been achieved by permitting religious leaders to influence the functions of the Ministry of Justice. A similar effect has resulted from incorporating a large proportion of the village mullahs into the service of the Ministry of Education as public school teachers.

This involvement with government has helped to disarm religious opposition to innovations. The deveiling of women in 1959 and the recent expansion of women's education have been accepted with virtually no organized religious opposition. By making the clergy an accomplice in modernization the government has largely won its support, although the capacity of the most traditionally minded mullahs to oppose more ambitious future reforms cannot be dismissed. To guard against this, considerable effort has been made to reorient the training of religious professionals, particularly in the specialized secondary schools and in the Faculty of Theology of Kabul University, toward a wider outlook and greater toleration of nontraditional values. The plans for creating a modern legal and court system embodied in the Constitution of 1964 open up both the prospects for greater modernization of the clergy and the widening of opportunities for the traditionalists to oppose the secularization of law.

Surviving Tribal Authority

The government has also found devices for ensuring traditional forms of allegiance from the tribes. In addition to the personal forms of tribal diplomacy exercised by the king and members of the royal family, the instrument used to provide continuity between the tribal, confederate relations of the past and the bureaucratic centralism emerging in the present has been the Loya Jirga. Historically this body debated momentous issues such as the election of a new king or the arrangements for ending civil war. As employed in the twentieth century, it has been an instrument for the legitimization of royal policies which intend to introduce new institutions or functions into the political system. Each of Afghanistan's three constitutions has been ratified by a Loya Jirga. The declaration of neutrality in the Second World War and the acceptance of the radical social changes introduced by Amanullah have been occasions for its convocation. Its membership is dominated by the major Pushtun chiefs, although other groups, religious leaders, and even influential urban personalities have been prominent. It provides the formal basis for the authority of the regime. Even so, its rather frequent use (eight times since 1900) does not necessarily suggest the perpetuation of localized tribal authority; the Constitution of 1964 provides that the parliament in a somewhat expanded form shall constitute the future Loya Jirga.

Some local tribal institutions continue to have significance for the political system. Several of the Pushtun tribes centered in the Pakhtia region which were instrumental in Nadir Shah's pacification of the country have retained special privileges and a unique place in politics. Informal practice has limited their obligations for taxation and military conscription. This reflects the considerable degree of autonomy they maintain. They continue to be important variables in the political system and the government's Pushtunistan policy has been closely related to the value of their political support.

Other tribal groups have held onto lesser degrees of autonomy. Moreover, to a considerable extent isolated village communities and the nomads have been able to remain detached from central authority. Both are difficult to tax or to impose legal codes or loyalty upon from the outside. Few of these remote communities retain significant political power; one possible exception is the large number of nomadic clans within the powerful Ghilzai tribe, whose base is the strategic Ghazni region. Bureaucratic authority can be expected to reach the most remote valleys of the Wakhan and the Hazarajat only rarely, but this incapacity has relatively little significance for the political system as a whole. Control over the nomads is a more serious matter, but it has so far been possible for loose surveillance to ensure their general allegiance.

The Educated and Professional Class

Since the establishment of Habibiya, Afghans in ever-growing numbers have received a predominantly westernized education. By the late 1960's about 500 Afghans had completed or done work toward graduate or professional degrees at foreign universities. In addition, several thousand had graduated either from Kabul University or the higher-level technical, vocational, or teacher-training institutions established since the reign of Habibullah. The great majority of these Afghans with modern education have pursued government careers, approximately one-half of them are employed by the Ministry of Education. School officials and teachers and officers of the Ministry of Interior are scattered throughout the provinces. Personnel of other ministries tend to be less widely distributed. Consequently, there is a large concentration of middle and higher-level officials in Kabul. The process of development of modern institutions in Afghanistan has virtually dictated that Kabul would receive the overwhelming share of the new facilities and opportunities for education. Thus although many government officials serve away from Kabul, the concentration of the most influential of the members of this class at the capital gives it considerable potential for political power. More than any other group that participates in politics, government officials, abetted somewhat by similarly trained Afghans in private professions or private employment, were the primary factors which induced the leadership surrounding the king to support the reforms in the new constitution.

The ability of this professional class to articulate its ambitions and its grievances has triggered the beginnings of change which are subjecting the political system to the most severe test of survival since the founding of the present dynasty. The professional-technical class monopolizes the skills and knowledge which are essential to expanding the authority of Afghan political institutions and the management of economic and technological change. To survive, the government must modernize. To modernize, it must create, employ, and support the aspirations of a modernized class with socioeconomic, and therefore political, ambitions. This has become a classical process among rapidly developing nations. Invariably it has led to broader, if not always democratic, forms of political participation.

The relationship of this emerging class with the other elements of state power is complex and as yet little understood. Membership in the new professional class overlaps with nearly all the other elements of power. The opportunities for foreign training, travel, and contacts which are the hallmark of professional status are being widely shared by all Afghan leadership groups. Thus, it is increasingly common for members of the royal family to acquire training and experience which coincide to a large degree with those of military officers, businessmen, landholders, bureaucrats, and even some contemporary religious leaders. In one sense the professional middle class has partially absorbed the older and more powerful segments of Afghan leadership. In becoming modernized all of the leadership elements have become more alike.

Lacking unity in its own ideological, professional, economic, and educational interests and experiences, the modernized middle class does not necessarily hold the political potential to eliminate the influence of the older elites. Its lack of cohesion tends to mirror the multicentered sources of power which have been typical of Afghan society. Increasingly, however, the future of the monarchy has become tied to the fortunes of this emerging class.

Expansion of Central Authority

From Ahmad Shah's reign onwards, would-be builders of the Afghan state have struggled to meet the requirements of stable government. The completion of this task under the Musahiban dynasty has coincided with a wide extension of the apparatus of government outwards in distance from Kabul and outwards in social mobilization from the political and cultural elites to ever-larger proportions of the rural population. Provincial and local administration first became functional under Zahir Shah; previously it had been essentially nominal. Tribal territories and tribal relationships are now subject to regional administrative jurisdictions. Tribal government has been progressively absorbed into provincial or district administration.

Signs of central control have become increasingly common. In some respects the process resembles a foreign intrusion. Hoary, largely autonomous local patterns of authority have been replaced by a bureaucratized, inexperienced, and centrally controlled administration which is staffed largely by a new urban, educated elite. Polycentered and partially democratic political forms have been replaced by monolithic authority. The process has run contrary to the traditional spirit and structure of much Afghan culture. The construction of a modern state has thus threatened some of the social and cultural roots which are vital to a sense of nationalism. To some extent, however, this threat was lessened by the realities which limit official authority in the provinces. As has always been the case, the government still exercises its greatest degree of control in the larger towns and more accessible villages. Greater technological and administrative sophistication now permits authority to reach farther and deeper into the fabric of traditional society. Despite this penetration, traditional Afghan institutions largely remain intact. The leading principles of Islamic law and local customs continue to challenge the secular concepts behind modern legal administration. Whereas tribal leaders now have less exclusive authority over tribal affairs, frequently these leaders have been employed by the government in unprecedented ways. They have often served as governors or leading civil or military officers in the provinces outside of their own home region. Such tactics strip the tribes of their original basis of independence, but they preserve the traditions of leadership in a manner which encourages national loyalty.

Under the Musahibans the Ministry of Interior and the army have been the primary agencies for more effective provincial control. The number of provincial and subprovincial units has tended to increase. The cadre of provincial officials, the governors and their staffs, has correspondingly grown and become professionalized. Senior provincial cadre—the governors, department heads, and technical specialists—are rotated from post to post, while their clerical, police, and menial subordinates are often permanent residents of the headquarters towns. Authority is established primarily through the exercise of police and magisterial powers. To a large extent, the governor is a policeman commanding provincial units of the national constabulary. As the senior local officers of the Ministry of Interior, provincial governors, subgovernors, and district officers supervise all local government activities, although the functions of the taxation officers and the local judges are to some degree outside their control.

With the widening in the 1950's of services in the fields of agriculture, education, and health the staffs and responsibilities of local government units have increased. Growing operational requirements have produced more elaborate administrative organization. Members of the governor's staff still remain answerable to him for local programs, but they must depend upon their parent ministries for funds and guidance, and it has become increasingly difficult for the governors to coordinate the programs and resources of separate ministries which frequently tend to compete rather than to cooperate.

During the earlier and simpler era of near total concentration on peace, taxation, and justice, relationships between officials in the provincial government were likely to be determined by personal and local factors. In most interior provinces little revenue could be raised. Taxation of land was light and even less revenue was collected from nomadic herders. Therefore, unless a province contained a trading center which made possible the collection of excise and, perhaps, customs revenues, provincial revenues often barely covered their own administrative costs. Partially for this reason prior to 1950 the central government was usually content with local operations that were self-supporting and that maintained order. This attitude left the provincial officials a great deal of latitude in carrying out their duties. Commonly this led provincial and local government to be associated with arbitrary and petty despotism.

In those provinces where tribal or intertribal organization was particularly strong, e.g., the Pushtun regions of eastern and southern Afghanistan, senior military officers with detachments of royal troops have frequently been assigned as governors. Much of the effort of these governors had been devoted to contact, negotiation, and participation in local tribal affairs. As the power of the government became more obvious, the military flavor of government in the tribal regions has given way to civil procedures.

Over the first twenty-five years of its rule, the Musahiban dynasty concentrated on perfecting a system which controlled the population. The impression generally given by the behavior of the local government was that its authority was to be neither resisted nor questioned. Corruption and incompetence in provincial and subprovincial government was inevitable, largely because the Ministry of Interior initially had little experience in staffing and supervising the scattered bureaucracy it employed. Under such circumstances when exploitation occurred it was primarily the result of government inability to control its own officials, not of deliberate policy. The accumulation of local grievances against provincial and local governments notwithstanding, the foundations of a regulated, systematic, and at least partially predictable administration were laid during the early years of the dynasty.

Some advantages became quickly apparent. The construction of roads (often carried out by conscripted labor —one of the most resented of local government powers) and the policing of the markets and trade routes gave impetus to trade. Regional systems of trade progressively became linked to national patterns and thus helped contribute to national consciousness. Moreover, the writ of one authority now ran completely, if irregularly, through-out the whole country. These achievements also made possible the apparatus by which the positive services of government could later reach the villages and tribes.

Contemporary Structure of Government

The rudimentary bureaucracy which tried to bring about social innovations during Amanullah's reign has been replaced in recent years by an administrative system capable of supporting and extending development efforts in all major fields. The creation of such capabilities has been one of the greatest achievements of the government since World War II. It can now shift its priorities from coercion to the development of social and economic services. Residents in the provinces are now availed of services which educate their children, improve their crops, protect them from disease, and inform them of national and international events. Often, these services are still seen as interferences with accepted and established patterns of life, but their qualities and their purposes add a new dimension to the significance of government for Afghan society. Major development efforts now cover every category of social, technological, and economic activity. Primary effort is in the classical fields of economy, education, health, and culture. In each of these fields one or more ministries are actively sponsoring a growing number of programs.

Economic development receives the greatest support. Agriculture has been divided into several fields of experimentation and development including irrigation systems, cultivation techniques, agricultural processing, promotion of export products, and the introduction of new crop varieties. Industrial development has also received a high proportion of investment especially in the fields of power generation, textiles, shoes, soaps, ceramics, food processing, and other types of light industry. With cement manufacturing and the beginnings of petro-chemical production, heavy industry is soon to become a major element in the economy. Transportation has made spectacular progress within the past fifteen years. Northern Afghanistan is now linked throughout the year to the Kabul region by a few hours of highway travel. Domestic airline service and radio and telephone communications complete a network which allows government and private agencies to co-ordinate activities on a nearly instantaneous basis.

Great changes have also taken place in education. By the end of the 1960's it is estimated that 30 per cent of school-age children were receiving formal education. The expansion of the school system has been accompanied by strenuous efforts to improve and extend the facilities for secondary and higher education. Kabul University is now a consolidated campus of nine colleges and more than 5,000 students. Between the elementary schools and the university has grown up a secondary school system and the development of several teacher-training institutions which attempt to keep pace with expanding demands.

Cultural developments are harder to measure, but the contact through Radio Afghanistan may have greater impact upon the lives of Afghans generally than changes in any other field. Several radio sets in most villages can now be tuned into the national broadcasting service.

Extension of health services has been slower. Most of the provinces now have hospital facilities, although few are hardly well enough staffed or equipped to be considered more than dispensaries. Gratifying results have come from public health programs designed to eradicate epidemic diseases. Advanced medical training receives high priority in the expansion of higher education, although a large percentage of Afghanistan's modern trained physicians go abroad for study.

These and other activities which are intended to improve and extend the capacities of Afghan society have required an enormous expansion of government. The number of agencies has increased and so has the extension of their services from the metropolitan region into the provinces. There are now fifteen ministries and one department of cabinet rank in the national government. Eight of these are concerned almost exclusively with developmental activities and two of the others maintain a balance between developmental and administrative functions.

Administration	*Development*	*Both Responsibilities*
Court	Mines and	Finance
Defense	Industries	Communications
Foreign Affairs	Public Works	
Interior	Planning	
Justice	Public Health	
Tribal Affairs	Education	
(Department)	Agriculture	
	Commerce	
	Information and	
	Culture	

Notwithstanding their rapid growth in organization, personnel, and funding, the developmental ministries tend to operate less efficiently and confidently than do the older agencies. Their administrative strength is diluted by inexperience and the rapid addition of new and often conflicting responsibilities. More significantly, for a government which must be concerned with the need to maintain basic authority, those agencies which generate its power still tend to carry the greatest weight in policy making. The foreign affairs, interior, finance, and defense ministries are also more effectively organized because their procedures have become more firmly established. Political questions thus tend to take precedence over development at the higher levels of deliberation. The combination of political caution with the difficulties of coordinating foreign assistance from many sources has created much confusion and frustration in the operations of the development ministries.

Developmental institutions have expanded beyond the regular ministerial framework. An impressive variety of such agencies has been created. The following list is not exhaustive: one national bank; two commercial banks; three specialized development banks in agriculture, industry, and construction; a network of government monopoly agencies which import manufactured items and retail them to the public; the Afghan Construction Unit which is active in structures and roads; Ariana, the national airline; the regional development agencies in the Helmand and Jalalabad valleys and in Pakhtia Province; the Rural Development Department which attempts to coordinate agricultural, educational, and health projects in selected regions; industrial concerns such as the Government Cement Company, the Jangalak Machinery Workshops, and the Afghanistan Electrical Company; the Afghan Insurance Company; new higher education institutions such as the Public Health College at Nangrahar near Jalalabad and the Polytechnic Institute which recently opened in Kabul; educational and cultural agencies such as the Education Press, which produces textbooks, the Government Press, the National Library, and the Kabul Museum; the Women's Institute which encourages social and educational activities; and such other specialized agencies as military and civil hospitals, the Red Crescent Society (affiliated with the International Red Cross), and the Cartographic Institute which is completing the aerial mapping of the country.

All of these organizations require officials with specialized education, frequently available only outside Afghanistan. Consequently, within the past generation a near explosion has occurred in the number and diversity of careers and the opportunities for related training available to graduates of Afghan secondary schools. The qualitative factors of manpower training, recruitment, and utilization have thus become especially critical to the performance of the development agencies.

Factors Affecting Administrative Performance

Under the Musahiban dynasty the cabinet has become the focal point of decision and action. Rudimentary cabinets existed as early as the era of Abdur Rahman, but only in the last thirty-five years have the prime minister and his colleagues occupied crucial policy-making and executive positions. This transformation was accomplished by Zahir Shah's uncles, Mohammed Hashim and Shah Mahmud. Mohammed Daud developed it further. With the acceptance of the king, Daud and his closest personal advisers monopolized virtually all decisions and control over foreign and domestic policy, personnel, and finance. During the Daud era, development programs began to require greater operational authority for the individual ministries. Thus, while Daud consolidated ultimate political authority, he progressively delegated the execution of policy to his ministers whose performance became increasingly sophisticated and vital to over-all government effectiveness. Accordingly, each major agency began to develop its own institutional individuality. Unique perspectives, practices, and structures began to emerge which created competition between agencies for funds, personnel, and cabinet influence. This decentralization of function facilitated centralization of final political control in the hands of the prime minister. The Daud government succeeded in reconciling one of the conflicting requirements of modern government: combining specialized functions with the consolidation of central control.

With the removal of Prince Daud in 1963, the tendency of government functions to become divided between separate and sometimes competing ministerial satrapies has grown. The multiplying demands of modernization have made the coordination of over-all policy increasingly difficult. The cabinet, which used to advise the prime minister and then carry out his decisions, has become the stage for struggles between ministerial constituencies over the priorities and decisions which determine policy. Whereas power was precisely located under Daud, since 1963 it has become divided among ministerial factions which sometimes represent private as well as public interests.

This division of power has not scattered evenly in all directions. As in the past, those agencies responsible for defense, order, foreign, and fiscal affairs retain the greatest influence. The power of the Ministry of Defense has grown with the strength it has acquired from Russian and Communist-bloc assistance. The Ministry of Interior has expanded through its control over the growing apparatus of provincial and local government. The foreign affairs and finance ministries have also enlarged their established roles: the former by virtue of the difficult task of coordinating foreign policy with foreign assistance; the latter through the added challenge of finding the revenue and credit with which to finance a growing list of public development projects while simultaneously funding routine administration. Both the older administrative and the newer developmental functions of government have caused political power to be retained by these four ministries. Although there has been a rapid growth in the staffing, expenditure, and operational sophistication in the development-oriented ministries, the leverage and influence which these younger agencies can bring to bear is usually less compelling.

This lack of political balance within the government may have been unavoidable given the rapid development of Afghan politics and administration. The political institutions are still in an early stage of formation. Their maturing requires a foundation of social and economic development. Politics and development became interdependent before the government acquired the experience to establish a balance between them. This circumstance adds to the difficulties confronting Afghan administrators, but it is the price which must be paid if the government is to carry out development while it is experimenting with new forms of political control and participation.

The tendency toward overcentralization of authority is

more evident in the operation of the individual ministries than throughout the government as a whole. Relatively little delegation of routine operational authority proceeds lower than the level of deputy ministers. Consequently, virtually all decisions must await the review and attention of the two, or perhaps three, top officials in each agency. Usually, several departments of equal standing report upwards through the deputy ministers to the minister. In addition to operational departments there are servicing and inspecting and even security departments within the separate ministries. Often the requirements of auditing and procedure dominate the functioning of the operational departments. Consequently, a great deal of overlapping authority and shared responsibility tends to plague government operations. The dozens of signatures required for ordinary personnel actions and the number of approvals needed before a warehouse can be unlocked are proverbial. The system stresses responsibility as opposed to authority, especially at the middle and lower levels. With decisions having to come from the very top, there is a general presumption that action is best protected from mistakes or abuse by the multiplication of paper work which certifies legitimacy of action.

Much of the cumbersomeness of the bureaucratic system has been created by the need to use employees whose training and experience have little relevance to government undertakings in the fields of development. Minute subdividing of authority can be viewed as a protection against incompetence and corruption; in the eyes of the minor official it is also a means of avoiding disgrace and punishment. Much remains to be learned about the sociology of Afghan government institutions, but it is clear that overcentralization often is the result of a rapid accumulation of demands for developmental services.

Despite increases in the number of Afghans with professional, managerial, or technical training, the number capable of performing at the higher levels of government has lagged behind needs. As is the case with political priorities, the most established ministries get a disproportionate share of the most talented administrators. This tendency works doubly against the newer development ministries: they can expect fewer talented administrators, while continuing to grow more quickly than the older ministries.

Rapid government expansion has also run afoul of other difficulties created by the limitations in trained manpower. Expansion has brought about a process whereby the age of a government official has become almost inversely proportional to the breadth, quality, and relevance of his qualifications for development responsibilities. Ministries and other agencies are hindered by the problems of placing and promoting younger and usually better-trained men within a system where the influence of the older officials is amplified by the traditional Afghan respect for age. There has been an understandable tendency to avoid the difficulties inherent in this problem by creating new agencies or departments to take over the administration of new projects or new phases of older projects. This device produces overlapping functions, often leaving the older administrative units with reduced responsibilities, but with enough continuing authority to interfere with the operations of the newer units. Thus, Afghan bureaucracy expands partially because of difficulties in integrating new operations, new skills, and new experience into the pre-established system. The cost in resources and clarity of objectives has been high. Nor can the cures for such bureaucratic ills be expected to come easily. Delay and competition between agencies—frequently at the cabinet level—are part of the price that Afghanistan is paying for its delayed attempt to modernize.

Government effectiveness is further weakened by the consequences of the meeting of Afghan social attitudes and practices with bureaucratic requirements. Nepotism cannot be considered a sin in a society which places family loyalty above virtually every other social value. Inevitably, recruitment and promotion within the government reflect desires to protect and entrench family influence. Little progress has yet been made at setting criteria for skills with which to grade official positions or to recruit new personnel. This failure is circularly linked to nepotism. The lack of merit-based criteria have allowed citadels of favoritism to become established, especially at the lower and middle grades. Those who have profited from nepotism or who fear competition on the basis of merit, particularly from recent vocational or professional graduates, naturally resist the imposition of standards that would put them at a disadvantage. The results have been uneven for the government as a whole. Each ministry has independently developed its own personnel policies, and it is generally the case that the stronger the ministry the more demanding are its personnel standards.

These institutional weaknesses also contribute to the prevalence of corruption. Despite elaborate procedures for review of bureaucratic actions, the collaboration of in-groups makes it difficult to limit conspiracies to embezzle or to defraud the government or to abuse the public. This difficulty is aggravated by the dependence upon key officials for planning and operations. These functions frequently include negotiation of contracts and the formulation of decisions which lend themselves to bribery and related forms of corruption. The contrast is dramatic between the size of the sums expended in development projects, especially those funded by foreign donors, and the pay scales of all government officials. Ministers receive salaries roughly equivalent to $140 per month, while the presidents and directors of the more important ministerial departments rarely receive the equivalent of more than $50. Clerks and other employees who maintain control over records and physical inventories usually are paid less than $20 per month. Thus, exposure to opportunities to profit from corruption to an extent totally disproportionate to their regular income places Afghan officials under strong and sometimes irresistible pressures.

Assessment of the performance of the Afghan government requires recognition of such limitations. It suffers not only from a lack of experienced and trained staff, but perhaps equally as damaging are the chasms between the values and attitudes of the social system upon which it is based and the demands of modern institutional development. From this perspective the rapid expansion of activity into new political, technical, and economic fields has produced some promising and some remarkable results. But it has spread manpower and institutional resources thin and some areas of activity have suffered disproportionately. Perhaps the most glaring example has been the inability of the government to implement legal reforms which are intended to guarantee rights under the new constitution. To be effective, judicial reform must take place at the local and provincial levels—a challenge to staffing and organization which the government does not have the resources to attempt. To a large extent, therefore, recent government performance is remarkable for what it has accomplished, despite the obstacles of political imbalance, overcentralization of authority, scarcity of suitable personnel, nepotism, and corruption.

Constitutional Development

With the approval of its present constitution in September, 1964, the Afghan government made its third attempt in the twentieth century to establish a framework for modern political development. Amanullah's 1923 Constitution was never enforced, but it and the 1931 Constitution contributed to the concepts as well as the circumstances which produced the new document.

Nadir Shah's constitution was drawn from Turkish, French, and Iranian sources. Some of its 110 articles were taken almost verbatim from the 1923 Constitution. Its internal contradictions were partially the result of this mixed parentage. The conflicts within the constitution stemmed from the attempt to combine fundamentally irreconcilable goals—the maintenance of royal control with greater latitude of action for other forms of political leadership; secularism with religious traditionalism; central authority with dependence upon tribal powers; and popular sovereignty with state monopoly of power. The resulting weaknesses kept the constitution from inspiring the allegiance of the modern educated and nationalist-oriented Afghans. As time passed, it was disregarded by both its designers and its critics, although it is possible that it did provide the framework for considerably more decentralization of power than had been attempted before it was abrogated in 1964.

The 1931 Constitution made plain that the dynasty of Nadir Shah had exclusive right to the throne. All essential executive authority was vested in the crown. Accordingly, parliament was created to be a consultative body having powers of debate and to be reflective of popular sentiment through direct election to its lower house by universal male suffrage. The somewhat weaker upper house was completely appointed by the king. Parliament was free to debate issues of its own choice, but had no means of affecting executive decisions directly. The king and his government had ample means with which to quash parliamentary opposition. He could declare an emergency, dissolve parliament, and promulgate laws by decree. Less drastic devices included royal veto of bills passed by parliament and upper house opposition to bills passed by the lower house. Provision was made for secret parliamentary sessions to which admittance could be refused to individual members. This made it possible for a parliamentary rump to act against the will of the majority.

The centralization of authority in the executive branch under the king was most positively spelled out in the provisions for a cabinet. The king was to appoint a prime minister who in turn selected his own ministers. As a group, the cabinet was subject to requests for information and explanation by the members of parliament, but the cabinet was answerable only to the king for its actions.

Considerable emphasis was placed upon the definition of liberal civil rights for Afghan citizens. They were entitled to free expression of religion, privacy of domicile and correspondence, free use and disposal of capital, and a set of protections guaranteed them due process in criminal justice. Torture and forced labor were not to be used as means of coercing or controlling the population. The state was committed to provide public education wherever facilities were available. Significantly, all of these rights were subject to the obligation of citizens to be obedient to and respectful of the government. By making rights dependent upon these antecedent duties and attitudes, the privileges and immunities of citizenship were largely theoretical.

Consistent with the policy of the dynasty in its early years, the constitution explicitly recognized the power and semi-independent status of the mullahs. Major legal questions were subject to the deliberations of an elite clerical council, the Jamiyat-i-Ulama, appointed by the king to advise him on religious and legal matters. Thus, while the constitution jealously guarded executive authority, it accepted the loss of control earlier forced upon the judiciary by Abdur Rahman.

In practice, the 1931 Constitution remained largely a façade for the continuing monopoly of royal executive and legislative control which was exercised by the prime minister. The structure offered some inducement to participation by secular intellectuals, usually within the career government service, and some members of leading Durrani families who had received higher education abroad. However, recognition of the knowledge and ability of the growing intelligentsia conflicted with the continuing requirement that politics be tightly controlled by the cabinet on behalf of the king. This impasse was not to be overcome within the framework of the 1931 Constitution.

By the middle 1950's the government was confident enough of its security to appoint former critics to important offices and to accept Russian assistance when previously it had minimized contacts with the Soviet Union. Changes in attitude on religious and social questions also marked a shift away from the original emphasis of the constitution. Prince Daud moved to weaken the political influence of the mullahs. If it had been thought advisable, there was considerable leeway within the constitution for political reform. The 1949 to 1952 period of political opposition demonstrated that parliament might have become more than an echo of the executive, if the government wished to interpret the constitution accordingly. Assessment of Nadir Shah's constitution must be qualified by the recognition that it was never fully put into force.

The Constitution of 1964

The reasons for Zahir Shah's decision to support a new constitution in the early 1960's are not yet clear. It may have been prompted by the political advantage of disowning a document which was identified with the autocratic posture exhibited by Prince Daud. The 1931 Constitution lacked clarity and consistency; more important, it offered little inspiration or guidance for Afghan aspirations toward greater democratization and modernization.

The king appointed a drafting committee of seven members, each of whom was publicly identified with reform, one of its members having been jailed for his opposition to the government in the early 1950's. For nearly a year the committee studied, argued, and composed, having consulted much of the literature on national constitutions. For the first time an Afghan constitution was written by a group which was not immediately controlled by the royal family, although the committee was undoubtedly sensitive to what it believed the king would accept.

Its draft was submitted to an advisory commission of twenty-six (original) members appointed by the king in the spring of 1964. This committee was drawn from all important elements of Afghan political, economic, social, and religious life. It included two women, several leading clerics, and representatives of the government employees, private business, the tribes, and the religious and ethnic minorities. The commission made modest changes in the original draft. Whatever royal influence was exerted on the constitution probably occurred at this stage. The reactions of the members of the drafting committee and other intellectuals in favor of reform suggested that there was relatively little royal intervention.

The final process leading to ratification took place in September, 1964, with the convening of a Loya Jirga whose composition differed considerably from that of previous assemblies. The selection of its members insured that popular sentiments would be well represented. The delegates included the 176 members of the lower house elected to the last session under the 1931 Constitution. A matching number of new representatives was elected by urban, village, and tribal constituencies. Through its press and its provincial officials the government attempted to make this election competitive and open. To the 352 popularly elected members were added 100 appointees: 34 (including 4 women) from among special interest groups, the 19 members of the senate of the previous parliament, the 14 ministers of the interim cabinet, 5 justices of the supreme court, the 7 members of the drafting committee, and the 24 surviving members of the advisory commission. The jirga thus represented virtually all elements of Afghan life, including non-Muslims, and it reflected virtually all variations of sociopolitical outlook, education, and experience.

It is likely that many of the delegates may have seen their responsibilities as an obligation to give the government what they thought it wanted from the new constitution. But as proceedings progressed, criticism and expressions of independent views frequently dominated debate. The 1964 Loya Jirga was a departure from previous assemblies which have debated principles of Afghan government. It was largely guided by the draft already prepared for it by committees which were themselves essentially free. The jirga modified the draft further, although most amendments were defeated. Despite past acquiescence in government demands, the debates within this assembly presented a remarkable combination of principles based upon the ideals of western liberal democracy and the spirit of Afghan traditional tribal councils.

Provisions of the Constitution of 1964

It is easy to underestimate the differences between the 1964 Constitution and its predecessors. There is a great deal of overlap with regard to the descriptions of the functions and powers of the king, cabinet, and parliament; the rights of the people; and the ideological rationale of government. However, in tone, in detail, and in articulation of democratic goals the new constitution is clearly innovative. Its preamble gives eloquent expression to a commitment to a new political era and a reliance upon secular authority for the underpinnings of the system.

IN THE NAME OF GOD, THE ALMIGHTY AND
THE JUST

To reorganize the national life of Afghanistan according to the requirements of the time and on the basis of the realities of national history and culture;

To achieve justice and equality;

To establish political, economic, and social democracy;

To organize the functions of the State and its branches to ensure liberty and welfare of the individual and the maintenance of the general order;

To achieve a balanced development of all phases of life in Afghanistan; and

To form, ultimately, a prosperous and progressive society based on social cooperation and preservation of human dignity;

We, the People of Afghanistan, conscious of the historical changes which have occurred in our life as a nation and as a part of human society, while considering the above-mentioned values to be the right of all human societies, have, under the leadership of His Majesty Mohammad Zahir Shah, King of Afghanistan and leader of its national life, framed this Constitution for ourselves and the generations to come.

These goals are expressed in the constitution primarily through the emphasis given popular sovereignty. Parliamentary and judicial institutions are to be strengthened to reflect the popular will and to ensure personal rights. The royal family's role in the routine operation of government is correspondingly reduced. The political process is opened to public view. The cabinet, which had previously controlled Afghan affairs in concert with the king, is accountable to a popular assembly, although ample provision is made for emergency controls.

ROLE OF THE KING

With the careful spelling out of the qualifications for royal office, especially the difficult question of succession, the king retains great residual power. He must be a member of the Musahiban family. Royal office is envisioned as symbolic of the unity of the Afghan people and the king is to be the custodian of the ultimate power of the state as it evolves towards a liberal-democratic system. Accordingly, while the king's authority originates in the constitution, he may disregard it. This prerogative is bluntly stated in article 15: "The King is not accountable and shall be respected by all."

His specified powers cover all aspects of government. The list includes appointment of the cabinet, direction of foreign and military affairs, appointment of one-third of the members of the upper house of parliament, appointment of all members of the supreme court, and the granting of pardons to convicts. The king is also entitled to dissolve parliament and call for new elections and he holds a veto power over all legislation. He thus has the means for assuming total political control in a manner which closely resembles the authority he previously exercised through his prime minister during the Daud era.

The contrast with the earlier constitutions lies in the alternative powers over policy and action given the cabinet and the parliament independently of the king who is expected to refrain from active participation in normal politics. This restraint of royalty from intervention in government is affirmed by the prohibition against political activity or the holding of high office be any member of the royal family except the king. While to some extent this provision, article 24, appears to be an attempt to prevent further royal dictatorship as was exercised by Prince Daud, its wider effect is to remove the royal family from the political competition and disruption which the drafters apparently expected would be inevitable in the process of democratization. By being put out of politics, the royal family is placed above politics.

RIGHTS AND DUTIES OF CITIZENS

A marked contrast between the new constitution and its predecessor is the enthusiasm with which the rights of Afghan citizens are defined. The injunctions to pay taxes, comply with the military draft, obey the laws, and respect the king remain. But virtually all of the emphasis in this section of the constitution is upon guarantees of rights and liberties. Echoing the Jeffersonian phrase, the Afghan constitution asserts that liberties are the natural possessions of the individual. This amounts to a rejection of the Afghan predisposition to judge behavior on the basis of group loyalties and responsibilities. The individual citizen is explicitly made the basis and recipient of liberty. His rights include movement, occupation, privacy of home and communications, as well as the classic liberal democratic freedoms of thought, expression, assembly, association (including the right to organize and join political parties), and the protections of due process. Positive rights, subject to the capacity of the state and society to provide them, are also promised in education, health, and economic opportunitiy. Citizens may seek redress from the state for unjust acts, although this right is held reciprocally by the state. The protections against the prevailing practice of forced labor are less clear. It is to be abolished and be replaced by politically accountable arrangements which are to protect the individual citizen while meeting the need for joint labor in the "community interest."

Altogether, the liberties and immunities make an impressive list alongside those of other liberal-democratic constitutions. In explicitness and in emphasis the authors have demonstrated a sincere commitment to the realization of such rights. Such a realization, however, requires more than the transformation of arbitrary government procedures and attitudes. More difficult is the necessity for an almost complete restructuring of the apparatus of justice and law enforcement.

Heavy moral burdens are placed upon the government in fostering education, health, and employment. These positive rights can take effect only with a vast expansion of services and a revolutionary improvement in the quality and quantity of trained talent within the country. Despite the difficulties which prevent their full and early realization, the rights expressed in this section comprise the core of the goals accepted by the government in committing itself to the constitution.

PARLIAMENT

The new Afghan parliament (Shura) continues the two-house structure of senate and assembly, respectively known as the Meshrano Jirga and the Wolesi Jirga. The Wolesi Jirga is to be the dominant body whose membership is based upon election by universal adult suffrage. Its 215 members sit for four-year terms, unless dissolution of the parliament requires more frequent elections. A plurality of votes from a single member constituency is sufficient for election to the parliament. The Meshrano Jirga consists of 84 members divided into three groups. One-third are to be appointed by the king, one-third are to be directly elected by provincial constituencies, and the remaining third are to coincide with the chairmen of the popularly elected provincial councils. Both houses have essentially the same freedom to organize and conduct business, but in cases of disagreement the Wolesi Jirga's decisions can only be delayed by the Meshrano Jirga.

Parliament has the right to exercise complete control over its internal organization, although provision has been made for an executive council in each house consisting of a president and a secretary and a deputy for each. Both houses are also expected to divide investigation, study, and preparation of legislation among internal committees. Members enjoy legal immunity for statements made in the course of carrying out their legislative duties, and parliament has powers of review should its members be arrested. Both houses have virtually unlimited jurisdiction over the areas of government about which they can take legislative action. The initiation of bills by members of parliament is a relatively simple procedure, although the constitution anticipates that much legislation will originate in the cabinet and some in the supreme court.

The exercise of these legislative powers is further encouraged by the requirement that parliament meet for seven months annually between stipulated dates. This clearly distinguishes it from the Shura established by the 1931 Constitution which only convened at royal pleasure. Parliament also has authority to investigate all matters within its wide legislative jurisdiction and to force the ministries to answer such questions as it submits to them. The seriousness with which these powers are to be taken is suggested by the provision that parliamentary laws supersede the principles of the Islamic Shariah whenever they are in conflict (articles 69 and 102).

Parliament offers a viable alternative to legislation by royal or executive decree, but the constitution also places important limitations on its powers. The limitations on its relationship with the cabinet are especially crucial and are subject to interpretation and evolution through practical usage. There is to be no overlap in membership between the cabinet and the parliament, a considerable departure from most parliamentary systems. A member of parliament must resign his seat if appointed to the cabinet. Selection of the cabinet is also beyond parliamentary prerogatives, although the tenure of the cabinet appointed by the king and the prime minister is subject to a vote of confidence in the Wolesi Jirga, a negative and clumsy procedure for the imposition of legislative will upon the executive.

Other limits on parliamentary power are also significant. While ministers are obliged to provide answers to questions submitted by parliament, once an answer is received the matter may not be pursued further. Formal debate of ministerial replies is not permitted. Perhaps more restricting is the provision for the automatic adoption of the previous budget if parliament does not approve the one submitted by the cabinet. Thus while parliamentary review and approval of the budget are real additions to legislative power, government operations cannot be halted by the failure to pass money bills—an important restriction on political leverage over the cabinet. Ample provision also exists for intimidating or, if necessary, dissolving a parliament whose membership has become dangerously hostile to the government. The king may disapprove parliamentary bills—thus permitting the cabinet through the king to have the last word on legislation. The Meshrano Jirga, whose members are more susceptible to government pressures, can be used to deflect or delay the will of a majority of the Wolesi Jirga. In times of national emergency, which could be linked to opposition within the parliament, the king has the unqualified right to dissolve it.

Consequently, within the new framework parliament has real power, but if it presses too hard upon the prerogatives of the executive it can be disarmed. The question of the degree of autonomy and effectiveness which can be developed by parliament is the crux of the democratic evolution of Afghan politics. Frequent or abrupt frustration of parliament could easily and rapidly lead to disenchantment and cynicism regarding the constitutional promises concerning popular representation and individual rights. On the other hand, parliamentary inexperience in using increased powers could lead to progressively more serious disagreements with the government resulting in the disruption or paralysis of the political process. In addition to the realization of citizenship rights, the constitution requires the growth of a parliamentary system within such channels as can assure both order and effective socioeconomic development. This is a tall order for any government and is particularly difficult for one whose experience with popular institutions has begun so recently.

THE CABINET

The cabinet, especially the prime minister, retains much of the executive power given in earlier constitutions. The prime minister is appointed by the king and he in turn selects his ministers who then must be collectively approved by the parliament in a vote of confidence. The cabinet exercises the wide powers assigned the king by the constitution. These include determination of over-all government policy on all foreign and domestic matters, the enforcement of all laws and judgments by the courts, and the development of programs which are to ensure security and economic and social growth. The constitution is silent on the functional relationship between king and cabinet. Indirectly through its stress on the symbolic role of the monarch, it implies that his executive role should be passive, except at times of crisis and emergency, but determination of when his intervention into cabinet activities is appropriate is left to his discretion.

The cabinet dissolves in the following circumstances: the death of the prime minister, his voluntary resignation, a vote of no-confidence by the parliament, the sustaining of a charge of high treason against the prime minister and a majority of the cabinet by the Wolesi Jirga, the dismissal of the government by royal decree, or by the expiration of the parliament's four-year term. The fate of a cabinet thus largely turns on its relationship with parliament. A considerable degree of harmony must obtain between them, if government under this constitution is to be workable.

THE JUDICIARY

The 1964 Constitution gives the judicial system status equal to that of the executive and legislative branches. Kazis had previously been largely free to conduct their courts without government interference. This freedom was supported by traditional practice and the vagueness of the 1931 Constitution regarding judicial powers. The drafters of the new constitution found the existing courts incompetent and disinclined to protect the broad range of legal rights which they wanted to have guaranteed. The need for reform was amplified by the testimony of many members of the Loya Jirga who cited instances of injustice and arbitrary decisions by the courts.

Two requirements were essential for judicial reconstruction: reorienting the courts toward support of the rights of individual citizens and reconstructing the legal system in order to make the exercise of these new liberties a practical possibility. Among the major areas of constitutional reform the judiciary presented the greatest challenge to the preparation of workable improvements. The gist of many of the complaints by jirga members was that the courts were already too independent and that this had led to corruption and injustice. Thus there was a strong inclination within the assembly to limit rather than to affirm the independence of the courts. Many members were willing to trust Ministery of Interior officials before they would turn to local judges for justice. The attitude of many who debated the constitution was thus radically different from the views which have led Western constitutional architects to separate justice from politics and administration. Proponents of the constitution, as it was adopted, have had to argue that substantial reforms could be initiated by the constitution within the framework of an independent judiciary.

The actual structure of authority and jurisdiction contemplated for the new judicial system is only roughly sketched in the constitution. At the top with total administrative, operational, and appellate powers is to be a re-created supreme court whose members are to be appointed for indefinite terms by the king, subject to ten-year reviews of their performance. It is empowered to establish whatever court system satisfies the needs for local and provincial justice and for manageable jurisdictions in the fields of criminal, civil, administrative, and military law. Virtually all the details of administrative and procedural reform were left to the Ministry of Justice and the supreme court—following its appointment by the king in 1967. Responsibility for criminal investigation and prosecution is to rest with the constitutionally created office of a national attorney general whose authority is to be separate from that of the Ministry of Justice.

In order to put together these largely undeveloped agencies much administrative and legal preparation was left to be completed. Among the problems of strengthening justice is the serious shortage of judicial officials with modern secular education. Clerical and administrative personnel competent to serve the courts are virtually non-existent. A heavy burden has been placed upon the Ministry of Justice with its responsibility for beginning the overhauling of the system. Perhaps the most crucial question is how rapidly and completely judges can respond to the changed foundation of jurisprudence mandated by the constitution. The principles and precedents of traditional law have now been relegated to a residual place as legal authority. Judges must expect to enforce a growing body of secular law based upon parliamentary acts, executive decrees, administrative regulations, and international treaties. Methods will also have to be found to incorporate the essence of both the Shariah and the customs based upon tribal and family law unique to the several distinct Afghan communities. At a minimum, the consistency and probity that will produce confidence in the evolving judicial system requires the codification and integration of these several sources of law.

Such a drastic reordering of the legal system will be an exhausting task. The scarcity of lawyers and jurists of broad professional training and background is likely to delay the completion for more than a generation. In the meantime it can be anticipated that the enforcement of the civil rights promised by the Constitution will be far from uniform or complete.

LOCAL GOVERNMENT

The constitution requires decentralization of government authority as rapidly as effective local institutions can be developed. It reiterates the 1931 provision for provincial councils which, however, are to be popularly elected, not appointed by provincial governors as had often been the case previously. Yet the duties and jurisdiction of these councils were left vague pending future legislation. They were expected to participate in economic development and to advise local officials on administrative policy. Once established, this principle of popular representation is to be extended to village government.

Despite the strong tradition of local autonomy and popular consultation within Afghan society, the attempt to bring formal instruments of representation and democracy to the peasant and nomad is an entirely new and experimental facet of modern political change. Accordingly, progress in this direction can also be expected to come slowly.

SPECIAL CONSTITUTIONAL PROVISIONS

Emergencies which would require the assumption by the king of all executive and legislative powers are defined as foreign or internally created circumstances which render the constitution unworkable. Upon decreeing an emergency, the king may dissolve parliament and abrogate —with the consent of the supreme court—the individual rights to privacy, property, assembly, and redress from acts of government. These suspensions can continue for no more than three months at which time a Loya Jirga must be convened for the purpose of acting to resolve the emergency. All measures taken during the course of the emergency must be approved by a newly elected parliament within one month after it is reassembled. Such fundamental rights as speech, movement, and association are not specifically subject to abrogation during emergencies. It is thus not clear whether the king, whose actions are not accountable, can act outside of the constitution regarding these rights, but the principle that the king is not bound by the constitution is actually implicit with respect to all questions.

No amendments to the constitution can be enacted during an emergency. In fact, amendment has been made so difficult as to create concern that inflexibility may prove to be a weakness. Either the cabinet or the parliament may initiate an amendment, but one-third of at least one house must take action. This step leads to the convening of a Loya Jirga, a majority of which must be in favor of the amendment. A parliamentary committee is then to be appointed to draft the specific amendment which must then meet the approval of a majority of the jirga and be accepted by the king. At this point parliament must be dissolved and new elections completed within four months. Based upon the new parliament yet another Loya Jirga is convened. Two-thirds of its members must approve the measure which then becomes law when signed by the king.

Only an overwhelming consensus could make such a process work unless the political realities made either the parliament or the cabinet a puppet in the hands of the other. In the latter case the spirit of the constitution would already have been destroyed and the question of amendment would be largely superfluous. The very difficulty of amendment could encourage cavalier manipulation or abuse of the constitution at times of crisis.

The powerful tradition of a grand assembly of notables expressed by the Loya Jirga is continued in the constitution, but its role and majesty are considerably reduced from their former dimensions. The jirga is to consist of the members of parliament and the chairmen of the provincial councils—once the latter are formally organized. Thus, for some years, in effect, the jirga will be the two houses of parliament sitting in joint session and it will always be controlled by the membership of parliament. Invariably, the jirga is to be called during times of danger to the country or the government. Specifically, the constitution requires it to meet to certify the abdication of the king and the election of his successor or the selection of a regent during a royal minority, to act upon impeachments of the cabinet or the supreme court, and to pass upon proposed amendments to the constitution. Normal parliamentary rules of procedure are to apply to its deliberations except that, unlike parliament, as a body it may act in secret. Authority and tradition are thus blended in the Loya Jirga, but it has no relationship to routine politics and its membership is to consist of popularly elected politicians.

The Beginning of a New Constitutional Era

The authors of the 1964 Constitution obviously intended it to lead to broader participation in the evolving Afghan political processes by all groups and categories of citizens. The sincerity of their search for the means to guarantee basic liberal rights, classical to the condition of democratic citizenship, also appears to have been genuine. To some extent it was possible to graft this document onto previous constitutional experiments and also onto the vestiges of democratic and egalitarian values and institutions in local and tribal life. But the events which have taken place since the ratification of the constitution suggest that the hopes of its authors were ambitious. Vital areas of politics must yet become institutionalized and routinized before the provisions for popular government can be effective. As structured in the constitution, the relationship between the cabinet and the parliament is almost invariably antagonistic. The absence of an overlap in membership can induce each branch to push for maximum authority at the expense of the other. The initiative for projects which might lead to further economic development can be expected to remain with the ministries, but a reluctant parliament has strong weapons for preventing the raising of taxes or the extensions of ministerial power which could be essential for program management. On the other hand, parliament cannot be safely ignored for the convenience of the cabinet. Such a tendency would frustrate the opportunity for widening the participation in modernization programs which representative government offers. Avenues of cooperation must be found to permit constructive parliamentary partcipation in development and all other primary political issues. The nonrecognition and nonenforcement of yet another constitution could lead to disastrous disillusionment and opposition amongst the growing group of Afghans with secondary or higher education who expect to benefit from liberal-democratic rights. Afghanistan's prospects for increasing prosperity and continuing stability thus require the achievement of evolutionary methods which will permit a constant, if uneven, progress in the realization of the constitution's main goals.

The evolution of the parliament as it comes to play an increasingly active and positive role in the total performance of government is not only to be determined by its potential friction with the cabinet. Internally, parliament needs to create the procedures which will permit growing legislative effectiveness. It began with almost no cohesion based upon political or ideological affiliation. No party organizations were lawful at the time of the first parliamentary election. Many issues left unanswered by the constitution require legislation. The fields involved include administrative organization, government personnel policy, regulation of educational institutions, controls over private and foreign investments, rules for elections, the organization of the judicial system, and the establishment of local government institutions. There are seventy references in the constitution itself to legislation which is required to make its provisions enforceable. Thus, at its inauguration in 1965, parliament faced an enormous task with little relevant experience.

Ironically, there is the strong possibility that the exercise of universal suffrage will strengthen the political power of the traditional rural leadership at the expense of the educated intelligentsia whose leaders were primarily responsible for drafting the constitution. The system of parliamentary constituencies based upon unrestricted voting rights and equal representation on a population basis limits the number of members of parliament who will be drawn from the modern educated class. With few exceptions they can only be elected from urban constituencies. Kabul, for example, has four representatives in a national assembly of 215 seats. Thus while the outlook and experience of the executive branch will tend to be urban and modern, the viewpoint of the majority of the parliament can be expected to be greatly different. It is likely that those Afghan leaders who intended the constitution to be an instrument by which the modern educated elite could control the broadening of the base of political participation, will find instead that conservative resistance to innovations, especially in the social and educational fields, has been resurrected by the powers given the Wolesi Jirga. During its early years the constitution must survive the need to improve the methods of modern development while at the same time a conservative legislature must commit itself to decisions which will introduce often disruptive innovations into national life. This two-sided requirement would present an exceedingly difficult challenge to any political culture.

4. The Economy: Internal Growth and External Aid

Afghan development efforts have become intertwined with foreign relations, especially those with close neighbors and the major global powers. Help has had to come from the outside for significant military, educational, or economic progress. Dependence upon neighbors has been aggravated by the loss of access to the sea early in the nineteenth century; until the introduction of air transportation, they have held hostage all Afghan prospects for external trade. A further disadvantage which Afghanistan carried into the present century was the almost total dependence of its economy on primitive methods in agriculture and animal husbandry. Exports were limited to fresh or dried fruits, raw wool and cotton, hides and karakul fur, and handwoven carpets. In short, the kingdom had little modern knowledge, a landlocked location, and an economy which offered products of only marginal value in modern international trade. Internal production was incapable of earning the foreign exchange required for effective modernization.

Afghanistan's internal trade, most of which was based upon barter transactions among peasants, nomads, and artisans, remained primitively organized and fragmented between villages and valleys which were largely self-sufficient. As a result the capital required for the initial stages of modern development had to come largely from income generated by exports. Limitations on internal capital and credit thus caused economic growth to become dependent upon international factors affecting foreign trade. Consequently, foreign policy has become closely linked to development prospects.

Dost Mohammed and Shere Ali found that coming to terms with the British on the defense of India and the pacification of the border tribes was the price of technical assistance for the royal army. Abdur Rahman discovered that British guarantees of protection could be easily converted into attempts at intervention, e.g., British demands for construction of military railways, telegraph lines, and fortifications, and the stationing of military advisers, all inside Afghanistan. Believing that military and economic developments when carried out by a powerful neighbor were incompatible with internal autonomy, he rejected such assistance. Since his time Afghan leaders have struggled to find a formula by which foreign help could be made consistent with independence and freedom of action.

Throughout this search, foreign policy and internal development have been subject to the crises arising not only out of the regional politics of southern, western, and central Asia, but also the global events which have determined the economic and political environment of the twentieth century. Both world wars brought serious disruptions to the frail and exposed process of innovation, even though the country remained far from the major theaters of conflict. World War II demonstrated Afghanistan's almost complete dependence upon foreign trade and assistance not only for economic progress but also for political stability. It was in this context that Afghan post-war governments have attempted to develop foreign relationships which could be utilized to support more rapid economic growth.

Internally the government confronted the rising aspirations of an increasingly sophisticated, educated elite whose own functions bore little relation to the nation's traditional economy. Effective economic reform required the integration of primitive and atomistically organized agricultural units with modern forms of trade, capital, and industrial management. Economic cohesion was to become as important an objective as economic expansion. Thus, in the past quarter of a century a method has been sought for combining politically disinterested foreign assistance with a simultaneous restructuring of the economy.

New Departures in Development Assistance, 1946–1953

Progress previously made in industry and commerce had been accomplished through the mobilization of private capital with government sponsorship and foreign credits. Private firms, largely with Bank-i-Milli support, had been able to meet part of the country's needs for refined sugar and mill-made textiles. Increased exports had made possible the purchase of foreign petroleum, tea, and consumer and capital goods. The wartime dislocations and the concentration of much economic power in the hands of a few business firms convinced some officials and intellectuals that the government should assert greater direct control over the development sectors of the economy. Since the early 1950's nearly all new sectors of the economy have been monopolized by the government, leaving sugar and cotton processing to private firms. This shift from private to public control has been closely related to the increasing emphasis placed upon building the infrastructural segments of the economy: facilities for transportation, communications, irrigation, power generation and transmission, and education. Such projects dominated development from the early 1950's until the decision was made to reencourage private development ventures in 1967.

The most ambitious task yet attempted by the government is the multipurpose water and land development and agricultural resettlement scheme commonly known as the Helmand Valley Project. Initial surveys and water diversion were begun by Japanese engineers in the 1930's. After the war the Afghan government, which held over $20,000,000 in credits from the sale of karakul skins in the United States, reached an agreement with the Morrison-Knudsen Company of Boise, Idaho, for construction of a comprehensive system of dams, canals, reservoirs, and power plants. The goal was to make the lower Helmand Valley into the granary which it apparently had been prior to the thirteenth century. It was expected that spring floods could be prevented and water could be distributed evenly for an additional growing season in the summer. Irrigation was also to make possible the cultivation of land which had returned to desert over the centuries. Nomads, especially those Pushtun tribesmen who make the lower Helmand region their winter headquarters, figured prominently in the plans for reclaiming abandoned land. Thus the project was ambitious and complex. It required combining the surveying, designing, and building of large public works with the training and resettlement of nomads and the adoption of new agricultural techniques over a wide region by a varied population.

It soon became apparent that Morrison-Knudsen's engineering capacity was merely one factor among several requirements for success. Before 1950 the original funds were exhausted with most of the engineering and construction work still incomplete and virtually no progress made in the actual irrigation of new land. With its reputation and most of its foreign assets committed to the project, the government turned to the United States for assistance.

Prior to the Helmand contract, Afghan-American relations had been friendly, but almost as distant as their geographical separation. The negotiations which led to American support of the Helmand project were to be the first steps in a long effort of the two governments to uncover methods of effective economic and political cooperation.

An Afghan delegation came to Washington in 1949 to request credits totaling more than $100,000,000 earmarked for completion of the Helmand Valley and related projects. Lacking the foreign assistance agencies that it has since developed, the American government assigned responsibility for discussing, designing, and providing aid to the Afghans to the U.S. Export-Import Bank. Negotiations between the bank and the Afghans resulted in a relatively short-term (eight-year) loan of $21,000,000 at 4.5 per cent interest. The Afghans were disappointed with the small size of the loan and its high interest rate. They had hoped that a series of transportation, power, industrial, and agricultural projects could be linked to the request for help in the Helmand Valley. The loan enabled Morrison-Knudsen to continue construction during the next two years. In 1952 another loan of $18,500,000 on slightly more liberal terms permitted construction to proceed further.

The Helmand experience was discomforting to both sides. The Afghans found American terms and conditions to be considerably less generous for neutral and economically inexperienced Afghanistan than was the case for nations whose foreign policies conformed more closely to those of the United States. The greater volume of grants and loans given Pakistan, Iran, and India usually on easier terms suggested that the Afghans lacked the political leverage to attract comparable support. The Export-Import Bank found the Afghan proposals to be unrealistic and backed by inadequate surveying and planning. Also hindering these early negotiations was the fact that American foreign aid policies regarding nonmilitary assistance were largely governed by conventional banking attitudes. As a result Afghans temporarily lost much of their optimism about American willingness to be an important source of assistance.

Added to these discouragements were the intrinsic difficulties of the Helmand project itself. It was launched before Afghans had had opportunities to gain skill and experience in planning, organizing, or executing less demanding schemes. Even in 1970 its value to Afghanistan's economic future remained uncertain. Most of the planned physical facilities were completed by the mid-1960's, but less progress had been made in adapting irrigation and cultivation techniques, crop selection, and sociocultural behavior on the part of conservative peasants and former nomads to the requirements for large increases in productivity. Much remains to be done in fashioning and coordinating further economic and educational inputs. Such efforts reach deep into the fabric of Afghan society; cultural responses have proved to be as important to the project as engineering feats.

In the early 1950's responsibility for providing and co-ordinating American assistance for the project was assigned to the International Cooperation Administration (ICA) which was superseded by the Agency for International Development (AID) in 1961. To date the United States has more than matched the $50,000,000 which the Afghans have invested in the Helmand. It has been the largest single program of American assistance in the kingdom.

Afghan-American relations in the early 1950's were also affected by the American refusal to provide military assistance. The decision was based upon the argument that no amount of foreign assistance could make Afghanistan defensible against a determined Russian invasion and that any military assistance would increase Russian hostility. Nevertheless, the Afghans needed help in modernizing their army and organizing an air force. Departure of the British from India in 1947 removed their largest source of military support and the Afghans were reluctant to become dependent upon Soviet military aid; Russo-Afghan relations had remained cool during the Stalin era. The truculence of Soviet foreign policy during the postwar years gave little assurance that Russian assistance would not lead to interference. After Stalin's death the Russian posture changed at the same time that Afghans were searching for new sources of military assistance. In 1953 both nations came under new leadership; Prince Daud took the office of prime minister convinced that Russian help should be sought.

A New Era of Foreign Influence:
Competitive Foreign Aid

The growing reliance upon economic assistance programs as weapons of cold-war diplomacy coincided with the establishment of the Daud regime. For the next ten years Afghanistan was given autocratic but vigorous leadership. The new government devoted itself primarily to economic development. Within a short time this shift in priorities was reinforced by increasing Russian and American interest in providing aid.

By 1954 the Russians had reversed their policy toward the new nations of South Asia. In place of hostility they began to offer economic and technical assistance and liberal credits for trade. At this point the Afghan government was particularly receptive to such a change in Russian attitudes. The Pushtunistan dispute seriously threatened trade connections with the Indian Ocean port of Karachi. The situation was a persuasive inducement for cooperation with the Russians who offered generous terms for the shipment of third-country goods across the USSR into northern Afghanistan. The Russians also offered attractive incentives for close economic ties. The first of their assistance projects in Afghanistan were imaginatively selected and highly visible. From the beginning they won a reputation for completing their work quickly, competently, and within estimated costs. Thus, for the first time in history the Russians were able to achieve substantial economic and political involvement in Afghanistan.

For its part the United States had committed itself in 1952 to continuing assistance in the Helmand Valley and the broadening of its foreign aid effort into such fields as education, transportation, agriculture, and technical assistance. Hence the stage was set for cold-war competition. Neither the Soviet nor American government has appeared to be interested in gaining a political or an economic monopoly. On the other hand neither has accepted the possibility of domination of Afghanistan by the other through default. Thus each created a presence by infusing funds and skills which grew progressively until the mid-1960's. A new chapter was added to the history of Afghanistan's survival between forces of overwhelming strength. Foreign assistance in unprecedented amounts began to change (literally) much of the Afghan landscape and swept the kingdom through several generations of technical and physical change.

Assistance also came from other developed nations. As part of its effort of re-establishment in world trade, West Germany extended large credits to Afghanistan for cement and new textile plants and a variety of consumer imports. Shortly after Russian assistance began, their protégés in Eastern Europe, most notably the Czechs, arranged to supply industrial equipment and military aid. Some European assistance, especially from France and Italy as well as Germany, represented a continuation of involvement and interest in Afghanistan that had begun before World War II.

Afghanistan combined a cold-war policy of neutrality with an assertion of identity with the nations of the Afro-Asian bloc. One consequence of this cultivation of third-world relations has been the growth of interest among several states in providing help to Afghanistan as one of the most disadvantaged nations. Among the twenty-one nations who maintain diplomatic representation in Afghanistan, nearly all are also providing at least modest forms of aid. This includes the United Arab Republic, Iran, India, Pakistan, Japan, and the People's Republic of China. Entering the field late, the latter has committed itself to a large effort involving nearly $30,000,000 in credits for agricultural and industrial development. Programs to improve education and health were of particular interest to the specialized agencies of the United Nations: consistent with Afghan needs, it has established one of its largest assistance missions in Kabul.

Accomplishments under Afghanistan's First Two Development Plans, 1957–1967

As the volume of foreign offers of help increased in 1955 and 1956 the Afghan government created a Planning Ministry to organize and coordinate development and foreign assistance. In 1957 this ministry was given responsibility for drafting Afghanistan's first five-year plan. It emphasized agriculture, especially irrigation, dominated by the efforts in the Helmand Valley. Over 40 per cent of the funds to be spent under the plan were intended for agriculture and related construction. Transportation and communications were to absorb nearly 30 per cent, mostly for paved roads. Industry and social services occupied relatively modest positions, each accounting for approximately one-eighth of the total. Small education and health outlays were mostly devoted to extending facilities from Kabul into the provinces. Improvements in coal-mining operations and some mineral and energy surveys were included.

This first plan put no emphasis upon integrating projects in the various sectors to reinforce and support each other. At this stage the government had neither the trained personnel, the statistical information, nor the devices for economic control which could ensure the dovetailing of the major elements of development. To a large degree such coordination was not as necessary at this point as it was to become later. In fact, the plan in its original shape and as later modified was governed mainly by the types of assistance foreign nations were willing to provide. This began a tendency which threatened to create increasingly serious problems in the later stages of development. Foreign assistance came to have a marked influence on the planning and performance of the development effort. Necessary as foreign help was, it tended to distract the Afghan government from creating a perspective of its own in planning and from mobilizing domestic resources.

Initiatives in determining the sequence of projects were especially affected during the early stages of Russian-American competition. The first Russian projects had the impact of demonstrating that short-term results could be achieved in contrast with the uncertainty of the eventual benefits to be gained in the Helmand Valley. In 1954 the Russians built a grain elevator with milling and baking facilities at Kabul. The elevator could store 20,000 tons of wheat to serve as a hedge against seasonal shortages and as a means of maintaining even grain prices. Ironically, most of the wheat which has been stored in the elevator has been American, but the identification of the Russians with its construction led to popular misconceptions about the origin of the wheat during the first years of operation. The Russians achieved even greater public impact in these early stages of competition by providing the credits, training, and equipment for the paving of the streets of Kabul, a project which the Americans had turned down as being of little economic value.

By the time that the first development plan had been designed, the Russian reputation for effective and apparently generous assistance was firmly established. As the Afghans projected future development they foresaw a growing volume of assistance spurred by cold-war rivalry. The Russians dramatized this possibility in 1956 when they offered a credit of $100,000,000 for road construction, industrial and power facilities, irrigation development, and a modern jet airport at Kabul. This offer included the construction of a spectacular paved highway through the Hindu Kush by means of a tunnel at the Salang Pass which would cut 150 miles and two days travel time between Kabul and northern Afghanistan. Later the Russians also offered financing and technical assistance in the search for petroleum reserves near Sheberghan. This additional credit included surveying, drilling, and equipment for extraction. The next major Russian move came with the agreement to construct an all-weather road from the Russian border through Herat to Kandahar, a distance of nearly 500 miles. The project, costing approximately $80,000,000, was secured by yet another credit. It alarmed some American and European observers who saw it and the roads the Russians were building in northern Afghanistan as attempts to gain both military and economic access to South Asia. The old fear of Russian convergence on the Indian Ocean was rekindled.

Virtually none of these projects were financed by the Russians on a gift or grant basis. The credits were based on long-term, low interest loans which the Afghans were to pay back through the export of such agricultural products as cotton, wool, vegetable oil, and preserved fruits. Repayment arrangements were to be based upon barter agreements established by treaty which committed a large proportion of Afghanistan's export capacity, especially from the northern provinces, to Russian trade.

In 1956 the first of several agreements for arms assistance was made with the communist bloc, primarily the Czechs. The first agreements, which were also based upon barter credit amounted to more than $32,000,000. Later the Russians came to take over virtually all military equipment and training assistance.

With the establishment of the ICA, American government assistance to Afghanistan began modestly in the fields of agriculture, surface and air transportation, education, and wheat commodity grants whose proceeds from sales to the local market were used to generate funds with which the Afghan costs of American-assisted projects could be financed. For American aid 1956 was also a turning point. From this date official American assistance, largely based upon grants, supplemented the earlier loans for the Helmand Valley project. Major road-building projects were undertaken to give Afghanistan better transportation links with Pakistan, partially offsetting growing Russian transportation connections. American assistance also quickly came to dominate the development of Afghan air communications. Pan American Airways purchased a 49 per cent interest in the Afghan national airline, Ariana, and helped to develop its managerial and technical capacity for domestic and international service. Beginning with DC-3's, Ariana added medium-sized propeller planes and by 1960 its service reached into Europe, the

Middle East, and South Asia. The Americans built an elaborate airport at Kandahar which was intended to become a major international servicing center. Several smaller airports were constructed with American help at the larger provincial cities.

American assistance to the ministries of agriculture and education dominated aid in these fields. Increasing numbers of Afghans received training abroad or through locally run programs. American participation in the building of a new campus for Kabul University complemented the older French efforts in law and medicine and German assistance in science and economics. The education, agriculture, and engineering colleges of the university came to depend primarily upon American aid for their laboratory equipment and professional staff.

Direct American assistance for industrial development began with commitments to improve the two operating coal mines in the late 1950's. Of greater importance was the technical and advisory assistance given the ministries most directly involved in development. Advisory teams participated alongside European, Russian, and United Nations experts in the planning, commerce, education, and agriculture ministries. By 1956 American assistance had reached an annual rate of $15,000,000. West German and East European assistance in the fields of industry, power, and communications also increased noticeably at the beginning of the first plan.

The emphasis on construction projects which characterized the first plan carried over even more forcefully into the second (1962–1967). Road building projects continued to dominate development expenditure and by the end of the plan more than 1,200 miles of paved roads linked all of the major regions of Afghanistan with Russian and Pakistani railheads. It was now possible to drive at high speed from Torghundi, north of Herat, through the Helmand basin to Kandahar, and then turn northward to Kabul and by crossing the Hindu Kush through the Salang Pass to reach Sher Khan Bandar on the Amu Darya opposite Russian Turkistan. Other paved roads connected Kabul with Peshawar and Kandahar with Quetta in Baluchistan, thus linking Afghanistan with Indian Ocean trade by truck and railroad connections. Furthur road construction continued after the plan. Herat was linked to the Iranian border in 1968 and a modern road connecting Mazar-i-Sharif with Kabul was completed in 1970. In the course of this construction the Afghan capacity for further extending the system of paved roads and for maintenance of existing ones was developed with both Russian and American help.

The existence and upkeep of the new road system has already had a revolutionary impact upon the Afghan economic and social systems. It has become economically feasible for goods of bulk value such as wheat and cotton to be moved long distances, thus beginning the integration of Afghanistan into one market system. Variations in crop yields need no longer create pockets of scarcity and glut in adjacent regions. Production can now be geared to national markets and crops and minerals can be brought over long distances into processing or manufacturing centers. Manpower has also become more mobile. Many transportation firms have been organized. Often they operate crude buses modified from truck chassis which carry overloads of passengers between provincial towns. The impact of expanded transportation has already been considerable upon the nomads who find that some of their commercial and hauling functions are being taken over by highway trucking. Rising distribution of manufactured consumer goods to the villages is stimulating greater diversification and commercialization in agriculture, especially in response to increasing urban demands for sugar and cotton. Limitations upon credit and marketing facilities, not transportation, are now the greatest obstacles to innovations in agriculture.

Power output also made spectacular advances during the first two five-year plans. Expanding at the rate of nearly 25 per cent per year, power generation increased from 47 million kwh. in 1957 to 288 million kwh. in 1967. This expansion was primarily the result of the completion of several large hydroelectric projects by the Russians, Germans, and Americans. Most of these had been located near enough to Kabul to service its growing industrial, commercial, and residential needs. By 1967 four dams, three with German assistance, had been completed along the Kabul River giving the capital region more than three-quarters of the electrical energy available in the country; actually more than the region could use in the late 1960's. Notable increases in power have also been achieved in connection with the development of the Helmand Valley and the new industrial centers at Mazar-i-Sharif, Pul-i-Khumri, and Kunduz.

With German help, telecommunications joined with the new roads and domestic air flights to spur economic integration. The development of public opinion based upon rapid dissemination of news and propaganda was now also possible. The Ministry of Information and Culture established a nation-wide network of news sources and news media outlets, connected by telegraph, telephone, and radio.

Quantitative progress within education was also unprecedented. During the first two plans the number of students in school increased from 126,000 to 540,000. The number of teachers rose dramatically from fewer than 4,000 in 1956 to 13,200 in 1967. Most of the expansion occurred at the primary level accompanied by construction of village school buildings, often with locally volunteered labor and building materials. In the most remote areas the formerly independent mullah teachers now operate what are classified as village schools. At these schools a government-supervised curriculum has been imposed on the three or four grade levels that are offered. A far larger number of primary-level students have been enrolled in the more elaborate official primary schools which cover the first six grades. These schools have permanent buildings and a staff with at least the beginnings of diversified skills and professional training.

Middle-level and secondary-level schools are enrolling a growing percentage of students in the eleven- to seventeen-year age group. While increases in the primary-level school population have slowed to 6 per cent annually, middle and secondary enrollments continue to expand at a rate of 25 percent. The attrition rate in the primary grades is enormous, although the rate of student advancement into the middle and secondary grades is improving. In 1968, 472,000 students were enrolled in grades 1–6; 55,000 in grades 7–9; and 13,000 in some forty high schools (*lycées*) throughout Afghanistan. In addition, students in vocational institutions including mechanical trades and crafts, art, business, secretarial, religious, and teacher training amounted to more than 14,000.

The magnitude of this expansion in all categories of education implies that increasing numbers of young adults with modern education are becoming available to participate in economic, political, and social activity. However, the process has been so rapid that there are serious qualitative limitations upon their skills. It has been impossible for the system to produce adequately prepared teachers in sufficient numbers to keep pace with the growing school enrollments. Almost one-half of those teaching in the village and primary schools have only completed the ninth grade themselves. Even among secondary-school teachers one-sixth have not studied beyond the ninth grade. Poor teacher performance and the great waste of student time, especially in the earliest grades, has been the price of rapid expansion. Even with the employment of many ill-trained teachers the ratio of pupils to teachers has reached levels which discourage effective instruction. In 1968 the national ratio of pupils to teachers in the village schools was 56 to 1, in the primary schools it was 43 to 1, and in middle and secondary schools it was 27 to 1.

Quality of education is further limited by the relative inexperience of Afghan educational leaders in developing goals and methods. This is reflected in rigidly centralized control over curriculum content, teaching methods, and the use of examinations and other forms of performance evaluation. Virtually all pedagogical decisions are made at the highest ministry levels. School administrators serve less as educators than as bureaucrats carrying out orders.

Teachers have little freedom to determine what or how they will teach. As a consequence, the system tends to produce students who have been exposed superficially to an ambitious variety of material. Primary-level students study at least two languages and a third is added in the middle or secondary grades. As many as fifteen subjects may be crowded into an academic year at the secondary level with the result that memorization and rote learning are the primary techniques of study. There is little freedom for the students to develop individual interpretations, approaches, or interests in the subject matter. Qualitative improvement is further obstructed by the shortage of textbooks and suitable readings in Persian and particularly in Pushtu—the latter being the mother tongue of nearly one-half of the students. To meet the growing needs of the schools the Ministry of Education has made strenuous attempts to produce and distribute textbooks and other types of instructional material. By the late 1960's textbooks were available for most subjects, but much work remained to make them representative of contemporary knowledge and effective instruments for learning.

Both the progress and the frustrations which have attended the effort to build a national educational system have important implications for the direction of over-all change in Afghanistan during the next generation. In recognition of this the United States, the United Nations, West Germany, and France have made educational assistance a major objective in their assistance programs. Much of this effort has been concentrated upon creating, expanding, and improving teacher-training institutions at the middle, secondary, and university levels. Teacher training at the middle level has been made available in most of the provinces. Higher-level institutions have been concentrated in Kabul, but Kandahar, Herat, and Mazar-i-Sharif have become sites for teacher training at the secondary level. Considerable effort has also been made to develop other vocational training facilities, many of these in conjunction with the operation of government agencies, e.g., military training, flight and mechanical training conducted by Ariana, and workshop programs run by the industries ministry. Vocational education, which is considerably more costly to provide, has become a vital alternative to academic education. However, a purely academic education leading to enrollment in the university and a chance for foreign professional or academic study is greatly preferred by students who are far enough along in the educational system to make their choices felt. One result has been a high rate of increased enrollment at Kabul University. At the beginning of the 1968–1969 school year the university enrolled 5,445 students, more than doubling the enrollment of 1962–1963.

This rate of growth is reflected by each of the ten faculties (colleges) of the university. All of them have received foreign assistance, but the faculties of Islamic law, medicine, science, political science and law, engineering, agriculture, and education have benefited especially. In addition there is an American team providing technical assistance for university administration. Aid from various sources in the form of foreign instructors and instructional materials has also been given the faculties of letters, home economics, and pharmacy.

The uneven accomplishments of the university after ten years of extremely rapid growth correspond with the picture at the lower levels of education. Virtually all university students suffer from the weaknesses of the educational system, although graduates of the older and more established Kabul *lycées* (Habibiya, Ghazi, Nejat, and Istaqlal, which receive considerable assistance from the Americans, British, Germans, and French respectively) enter the university comparatively well prepared. The choice of languages for instruction and study remains difficult. Afghan students who reach the university level are expected to have a working knowledge of one European language, in addition to Persian and Pushtu. Such competence is rarely achieved in the schools and at the university level the student faces an environment which is divided by language at least six ways. Much of the instruction is given in French, German, English, or Arabic by the foreign instructors furnished by the assistance programs. Throughout the 1960's approximately a hundred foreign professors were on the campus and their number increased with completion of the Russian-supported Polytechnic (university-level) Institute in 1968. University students consequently must contend with lectures in at least one foreign language over which they usually have poor conversational command. The linguistic variety makes the achievement of unified administration and a unified university community extremely difficult. Foreign teaching methods and educational philosophies tend to be adopted severally by the Afghans who are separated from each other by distinct campus units and foreign academic assistance programs. Kabul University has the large task of generating a sense of academic and intellectual identity in the midst of a Babel of foreign tongues.

American assistance has made possible one significant step toward unification. A single physical campus was completed in 1963. It consists of modern classroom and service buildings and a large dormitory complex for the housing of students from the provinces. Included is a modern college library which offers a focal point for campus unity. The library collection, however, demonstrates yet another important impediment to satisfactory student performance at the university. Because they are primarily from American sources, most of the 100,000 volumes in the library are in English, although a large proportion are in French or German. Only about 20 per cent of the collection is in Persian or Pushtu. Despite the emphasis placed upon foreign language at the high-school level, few Afghan students at the university are equipped to profit from college-level textbooks in European languages.

The factors which have combined to limit Afghan educational development have inhibited qualitative changes more severely than quantitative growth. It has been easier to increase the number of students at all levels than to improve their education. Many of the most promising of the university students and some graduates from the stronger *lycées* are sent abroad on grants or scholarships. Such opportunities offer the greatest chance for careers at the highest levels of government service or in the modern professions. Between the limitations on quality which circumstances have imposed on higher education in Afghanistan and the rapid pace of economic and political change, student ambitions have increased more quickly than their qualifications. As a result there has been growing student dissatisfaction with school conditions and increasing political activism.

Major advances in health care have also brought change to Afghanistan. Equipment and facilities for both preventive and curative services have been increased primarily through United Nations support with some private foreign help. Malaria has been eradicated, and immunization against tuberculosis, cholera, and smallpox has brought such endemic diseases much closer to effective control than was conceivable in the early 1950's. Nearly 1,000 Afghan physicians have received modern medical training either at Kabul University, at the new medical college near Jalalabad, or abroad. The Ministry of Health has constructed hospital and health facilities at most provincial capitals and has set up mobile teams to provide medical services, including immunization, for the more remote villages and the nomads.

Intestinal diseases continue to take a heavy toll of Afghan lives and health. Because of the prevalence of dust in the dry climate, trachoma and other eye diseases are common. Dysentery is believed to be the largest cause of death in small children. No Afghan city has established a system of pure drinking water and sewage systems are nonexistent. Despite growing urbanization, health standards have been slow to improve. However, if the plans for increasing industrialization and modern tourism are to materialize in the near future, significant strides in public health will be crucial. Many of the necessary skills and facilities are now available in Kabul, but modern public health and curative facilities remain woefully inadequate throughout the rest of the country.

Increases in Production, 1957–1967

Impressive as have been many of the advances in power generation, transportation, communications, education, and health the first two plans provided few direct increases in production. They concentrated less on production than on creating a basis for it. Even so, there were some notable advances in both industrial and agricultural output. There were also cases of stagnation and even decline which suggest that the next phase of development will be characterized by increasingly difficult managerial problems of resource allocations and the integration of production and marketing. (See economic development data in tables 2, 3, and 4.)

Large increases in industrial production occurred with the establishment of new cement and textile factories and facilities for vegetable oil extraction. Largely with American help, the output of the coal mines increased from 66,000 to more than 150,000 tons. There were also increases in the production of processed cotton and sugar, but neither reached planned levels. In both fields imports continued to dominate consumption. The value of sugar imports climbed from $1,200,000 in 1963 to $5,300,000 in 1967, while the total cost of cotton and other imported textiles remained virtually the same at about $8,500,000. Afghan industry was still incapable of supplying consumer goods except for some textiles and leather goods and handcrafted household items.

Agricultural production improved, but unevenly. Despite efforts to increase the amount of irrigated land, acreage available for cultivation remained at approximately 7,800,000 hectares throughout the 1960's. Wheat was still the primary crop, although its acreage dropped 12 per cent over the five years ending in 1967. Wheat output, however, remained steady with small annual rises and declines; productivity—particularly low in Afghanistan—is recorded to have increased from 0.8 to 1.1 tons per hectare. Output patterns in rice and corn, the other two major grains, were similar with gradual rises in productivity against small reductions in the area sown. Output of raw cotton proved to be especially disappointing. After a decade of increases, cotton production began to decline in 1963. Land under cotton decreased from 74,000 hectares to 48,000 by 1966 and production, after peaking at 110,000 tons, dropped to below 70,000 in 1966 and only partially recovered in 1967. This decline reflected the difficulty experienced in inducing farmers to transfer land under grain to cotton. Unfavorable prices set up by the government discouraged cotton planting causing shortages of raw material for the mills. Sugar beet and cane production experienced very gradual rises in the 1960's primarily on the basis of modest acreage increases. Even so, not enough raw sugar has been available to employ the refinery in Baghlan province for more than several weeks per year.

Fruits and vegetables experienced the greatest growth. In the five years ending in 1967 the output of grapes, apricots, apples, melons, and pears increased by 150 per cent, almost entirely on the basis of increase in area cultivated. Favorable prices for fruit drew land away from grain and other staple crops. Even so, the amount of land under orchards reached only 135,000 hectares, less than 2 per cent of the total land under cultivation. Greater fruit production resulted in the increase of exports in fresh and processed fruit from 46,000 to 110,000 tons between 1963 and 1967. Vegetable production increased by 20 per cent entirely due to improvements in productivity, the area devoted to vegetables having decreased by 9 per cent.

Table 2. Industrial production in Afghanistan, 1963–1970

Item	1963–64	1964–65	1965–66	1966–67	1967–68	1968–69	1969–70
Electricity (kwh.)	181,336	203,616	286,248	302,298	298,278	317,409	324,000
Natural Gas (million cubic meters)					342	1,681	2,029
Coal (tons)	99,200	112,700	144,000	161,600	151,000	124,800	136,200
Cement (thousand tons)	103,300	142,200	172,200	174,000	123,600	90,600	103,400
Salt (tons)	31,700	29,500	38,100	38,700	31,300	36,900	36,600
Lapis Lazuli (thousand kilos)	10,800	5,000	8,600	10,300	5,500	N.A.	4,500
Shoes (pairs)	57,000	52,900	74,800	107,600	123,300	123,800	161,100
Cotton Yarn (thousand bundles)	208,600	177,800	239,400	245,200	193,300	80,300	91,000
Cotton fabric (million meters)	36.9	47.0	55.2	66.0	64.0	48.7	49.2
Woolen fabric (meters)	200,000	213,000	305,000	463,000	443,000	445,800	663,400
Rayon (meters)	300,000	700,000	1,000,000	1,304,000	1,311,000	2,817,700	2,519,800
Sugar (tons)	7,000	3,900	7,400	7,100	7,500	5,300	7,600
Manufacturing index (1965–66 = 100)	75	87	100	106.5	99.9	87.2	N.A.

Sources: Royal Government of Afghanistan, Ministry of Planning, Department of Statistics, Survey of Progress, 1968–69 (Kabul, 1969), p. S–21; and Survey of Progress, 1969–70 (Kabul, 1970), p. S–24.

Table 3. Summary of Afghanistan's balance of trade, 1957–1969 (in dollars)

Year	Value of commercial exports	Value of commercial imports	Net commercial balance	Foreign aid imports
1957–58	58,860,700	47,179,900	11,680,800	10,293,700
1958–59	46,401,600	52,091,500	(5,689,900)	20,666,100
1959–60	60,361,900	45,058,300	15,303,600	35,880,200
1960–61	49,885,300	49,177,800	707,500	37,620,500
1961–62	53,389,700	49,107,400	4,282,300	49,986,900
1962–63	58,891,700	59,387,500	(495,800)	56,532,900
1963–64	68,989,500	61,902,700	7,086,800	63,807,000
1964–65	70,680,000	66,850,000	3,830,000	74,520,000
1965–66	69,970,000	56,510,000	13,460,000	74,470,000
1966–67	64,670,000	66,680,000	(2,010,000)	101,500,000
1967–68	66,400,000	62,930,000	3,470,000	75,430,000
1968–69	71,800,000	65,560,000	6,240,000	63,160,000
1969–70	*81,430,000	N.A.	N.A.	54,200,000
	* preliminary			
Totals (to 1969)	740,300,400	682,435,100	57,865,300	663,867,300

Sources: Royal Government of Afghanistan, Ministry of Commerce, *Afghanistan's Foreign Trade, 1335–1342 (1956–1964)* (Kabul, 1965), Table 2; Royal Government of Afghanistan, Ministry of Planning, Department of Statistics, *Survey of Progress, 1968–1969* (Kabul, 1969), pp. S–14 and 18; and *Survey of Progress, 1969–70* (Kabul, 1970), pp. S–10, 13, 14.

These statistics are subject to adjustment and do not indicate foreign services rendered Afghanistan abroad, i.e., imports for the purposes of balance-of-payments accounting. These have averaged approximately $1,350,000 annually since 1963.

The difference between the net commercial balance of payments earned by Afghanistan and the goods and services accumulated through foreign aid imports (amounting to a disparity of $606,002,000 during the twelve-year period ending in 1969) gives a rough indication of the degree of dependence which Afghanistan's economic development had come to have upon foreign assistance.

Table 4. Recent foreign assistance to Afghanistan by source (in dollars) (commodity assistance not computed)

Donor	Total aid before 1967	Aid, 1967–68	Aid, 1968–69	Aid, 1969–70	Cumulative Total
U.S.S.R.	568,100,000	44,720,000	30,520,000	28,400,000	661,740,000
Grants	94,400,000		6,300,000	5,800,000	106,500,000
Loans	473,700,000	44,720,000	24,220,000	22,600,000	565,240,000
U.S.A.	387,900,000	12,730,000	4,790,000	1,440,000	406,860,000
Grants	310,300,000	6,670,000	2,810,000	860,000	320,640,000
Loans	77,600,000	6,060,000	1,980,000	580,000	86,220,000
West Germany	73,400,000	7,640,000	6,470,000	2,300,000	89,810,000
Grants	2,300,000	1,700,000	1,900,000	890,000	6,790,000
Loans	70,100,000	5,940,000	4,570,000	1,410,000	82,020,000
United Nations	21,640,000	980,000	2,110,000	6,240,000	30,970,000
Grants	21,640,000	980,000	700,000	2,080,000	25,400,000
Loans			1,410,000	4,160,000	5,570,000
Peoples Republic of China (all loans)	15,300,000	2,980,000	5,530,000	5,560,000	29,370,000
All Sources	1,095,400,000	69,050,000	50,200,000	44,210,000	1,258,860,000
Grants	428,400,000	9,350,000	12,250,000	9,720,000	459,720,000
Loans	667,000,000	59,700,000	37,950,000	34,490,000	799,140,000

Sources: Royal Government of Afghanistan, Ministry of Planning, Department of Statistics, *Survey of Progress, 1968–69* (Kabul, 1969), p. S-2; USAID/Afghanistan, *Briefing Book, January 1970* (Kabul, 1970), pp. 34, 35.

The table incorporates some interpolations. Figures occasionally inconsistent for last five digits because of rounding.

Despite scattered gains, agricultural shortfalls at the end of the second plan demonstrated that the organization and technical employment of resources had not kept up with the growth of Afghan needs. Increases in demand for agricultural products caused by population growth and rises in commercial-industrial needs were not being met. Annual deficits in wheat which had averaged between 50,000 and 100,000 tons in the late 1950's and early 1960's were expected to reach 150,000 tons or more by the

late 1960's. The shortfalls in cotton were especially disappointing. Thus agricultural productivity remained a critical, but doubtful, factor for further over-all economic
progress.

Notable changes in the livestock population were recorded between 1963 and 1968, especially for sheep. Fat-
tailed sheep are estimated to have increased by 3,000,000
head to 15,000,000. Of greater importance for export
earnings was the nearly 1,500,000 head increase estimated
in the population of karakul sheep. Productivity in both
karakul pelts and sheep wool is tied to problems of
quality. Improvements in fodder, genetic standards, shear-
ing techniques, disease prevention, cleaning, and grading
remain the major obstacles to greater value of output
from animal husbandry.

Directions in Foreign Trade and Foreign
Assistance since 1967

During the first two plans Afghan exports modestly
increased in value, but the performance of individual
export products was sporadic and uneven. Moreover, de-
pendable returns from the agricultural commodities which
account for more than 90 per cent of the value of Afghan
exports were impossible because of wide fluctuations in
world prices over which Afghans had little control. Carpet
production, which dominated nonagricultural exports,
was plagued by problems of quality standards and strong
foreign competition. Thus, Afghan ability to earn foreign
currency remained almost totally dependent upon the segments of the economy which have been exposed to peril-
ous world market conditions and which suffer from qualitative disadvantages. Few of the export products other

than fresh and processed fruits, nuts, and vegetables have experienced consistent and important increases in value. Raw cotton underwent a notable decline as a result of lost acreage and raw wool exports started declining in value in the late 1950's. Consequently, while Afghanistan has been able to maintain a modestly favorable trade balance (exclusive of the funds, commodities, and services imported into the country through the financing of foreign assistance programs) it has not been sufficiently favorable to support self-generating development.

A large proportion of imports is not contributing to productivity. Considerably more than one-half of the value of imports has been attributable to consumer instead of capital goods. Changes in consumption tastes and habits which have accompanied urbanization and modernization are developing much faster than is domestic production of consumer goods. One of the risks incurred in concentrating upon development of the economic infrastructure during the first two plans was that while they generated income from foreign goods and services and the employment of Afghans on construction projects, they did little to put domestically produced consumer goods on the market. Consequently, the money supply increased far more rapidly than did the supply of either manufactured goods or food. Rising demands for goods which Afghanistan must import began to distort the allocation of development resources. Increases in the prices of subsistence goods, especially wheat, threatened to create serious economic and political problems. The urban working force is the segment of the population most directly affected by inflation. Economic alienation of government workers and the mushrooming number of manual laborers who have migrated to the cities have become growing political concerns.

Further development of foreign trade will be closely linked to the magnitude and quality of foreign assistance. Foreign aid reached a level of $100,000,000 per year at the end of the second five-year plan when construction on the large road and dam-building projects was at its peak. Since 1967 aid has declined sharply. By 1968–1969 the value of imports based upon foreign assistance had dropped below $60,000,000 and immediate future prospects suggest further reductions. Simultaneously, there has been a progressive increase in the cost of servicing and repaying the foreign loans which have accumulated. In 1970 such costs had risen to more than 40 per cent of the assistance which Afghanistan was receiving. Thus, with the shrinking of the net input of foreign capital into the economy after the end of the second plan, Afghanistan's exports have been forced to play an increasingly important role in generating capital for development.

Other changes in foreign assistance include the drastic decline of American aid since 1966, the growing preponderance of Russian aid, and the recent emergence of international assistance agencies, particularly the World Bank, as major donors. By the late 1960's cumulative Russian aid had reached considerably more than $600,000,000 and during the years 1967–1970 the value of Russian assistance approximated 70 per cent of the aid from all sources. Closely related to this dependence upon the Russians has been the growing importance of loans. In the five years following 1962 the proportion of foreign assistance from all sources in the form of grants dropped from 60 to 20 per cent. In 1966, of the more than $81,000,000 in commitments made by foreign donors, less than $10,000,000 was in grants. This trend is related to the increasing tendency of the Russians to make loans. Since 1964 over 70 per cent of the capital they have made available has been loaned.

Even more striking has been the decline in the share of American assistance. It accounted for more than one-third of the aid received by Afghanistan through 1967. For 1967 the American share had dropped to one-fifth and in 1969 to about 3 per cent, a lower rate than the assistance given by Communist China, the United Nations, and West Germany. As their total international assistance effort has been cut back, the Americans have also converted a large share of their assistance to Afghanistan from grants to loans.

One necessary response of the Afghan government to this drying up of assistance sources has been to commit itself to long-term loan agreements, mostly with the communist bloc and the West Germans. The resulting burden can only have a profound effect upon the content and direction of Afghanistan's foreign trade and the pace of over-all internal economic development. To some extent the economy has been able to absorb greater foreign debts. Since 1967 the export of natural gas to the USSR has become an important source of export income reaching a value of nearly $10,000,000 in 1968. Even so, Afghan agriculture and industry must expand greatly before export earnings can be expected to catch up with the accumulating amounts due from loans. Unfortunately, much of the added productive growth which is required must rely upon a high level of continuing foreign aid.

Greater interest in Afghanistan's development opportunities and problems has recently been exhibited by international banking institutions, which have become increasingly capable of providing capital and technical assistance. Together with the United Nations Development Program such agencies currently offer expanding sources of assistance. The International Bank for Reconstruction and Development (World Bank) has been particularly active. In the late 1960's it made loans of more than $13,000,000 to Afghanistan for the construction of schools, the maintenance of roads, and the establishment of an agricultural development bank. The Asian Development Bank has committed itself to programs encouraging more effective use of irrigation facilities and it is conducting surveys for potential loans. The International Monetary Fund provided support for Afghan foreign exchange reserves by more than $8,000,000 in loans to the Central Bank. Thus, Afghanistan can reasonably expect to have continuing help, both on bilateral and international bases as the development effort moves into a fourth plan in 1972. However, the era of foreign help stimulated by cold-war competition in the hope of winning political influence and diplomatic leverage appears to be largely over. As competitive giving passes so has the originally primitive condition of the economy which had made bilateral construction projects so dramatic and appealing. By the mid-1960's the pace of internal development was to be increasingly governed by how effectively the roads, electricity, irrigation systems, and school graduates could be used to generate greater production and thus add to the stocks of domestic capital needed to fuel progressively more sophisticated and complex stages of growth.

The Legacy of Early Development Progress:
The Need for Economic Integration

By 1964 the strains and imbalances in the Afghan economy partially caused by large infusions of foreign capital and the rapid pace of development had produced serious problems of economic management. Foreign assistance was making possible the importation of goods and services at a rate roughly twice the Afghan capacity to earn foreign exchange through exports. This not only created an accumulating foreign debt, it was also putting disruptive pressures on the internal economy. The most obvious danger was price inflation serious enough to neutralize efforts to raise domestic capital and to put a severe price-wage squeeze on the government officials, teachers, and technicians whose roles were critical for the successful completion of development projects. Inflation also threatened to transfer private capital into nonproductive investments such as urban real estate and the hoarding of agricultural commodities, thus further stimulating price increases.

Despite government attempts to limit consumer imports such commodities persistently absorbed 75 per cent of the value of all imported goods between 1963 and 1968. Large efforts and outlays for development were being rendered useless by market trends which were permitting most of the new wealth created by development to be wasted upon nonproductive consumption. This tendency threatened to prevent effective use of the infrastructure as the means for increasing production and a wider distribution of goods and economic opportunities. Inflation and dependence upon foreign consumer goods could be expected to prevent the economy from becoming capable of meeting internal demand, leading to an indefinite period of dependence upon foreign assistance.

The government responded to inflation and its attendant dangers by attempting to limit the supply of credit and money. Between 1963 and 1967 this policy resulted in virtually no increase in direct government expenditure on development projects. While the operational costs of administration did increase, particularly for education, a serious effort was made to restrict deficit budgeting. During this period the government debt to the internal banking system actually declined. Monetary stability was demonstrated by the steadiness in the value of the Afghan currency in terms of the dollar and the British pound. The government also took several steps to increase its revenues through more effective collection of established taxes and a slight broadening of the base of taxation especially from individual and corporate income.

One of the short-term effects of these attempts to reduce inflationary pressures was to discourage the volume of private investment. The internal economy experienced a period of stagnation. Obviously, therefore, one of the primary challenges facing the government at the beginning of the third plan (1967) was the need to find a strategy which would balance investment incentives against the danger of rapid inflation.

Failure to integrate the expanding sectors of the economy has been another constraint upon development. To some extent it had been possible to complete ambitious construction projects without a high degree of coordination either in execution, which was often undertaken by separate foreign agencies, or in their contribution to the total economy. Roads and schools and dams could be built and men trained to construct them without initial concern for how they were to fit together once they were operational. The emphasis on infrastructure had permitted large segments of development to take place autonomously. Near the end of the second plan it became apparent that their usefulness had come to depend upon the degree to which they meshed into an economy which could service them as well as profit from their operations. The performance of the modern segments of the economy was vulnerable to the stoppages caused by failures to allocate and coordinate scarce human, material, or financial resources. The scope of projects which could be sustained ultimately depended upon inputs from Afghan sources. Management, manpower, public and commercial services, systematic priorities and political support, all were essential and most are governed exclusively by internal factors. The quality of their combination almost entirely depends upon Afghan leadership.

The managerial challenge includes serious and growing problems of manpower allocation. Effective utilization of large numbers of foreign technicians still is required. Considerably more difficult is the need to refashion the educational system to enable it to produce graduates with the skills required by the evolving economy. Between the mass of illiterate and uneducated peasants and nomads on the one hand and the several hundred Afghans with graduate degrees on the other, there lies the immense need for the technical and craft skills essential for permanent economic progress. Thus the training of skilled workers (foremen, technicians, engineers, chemists, agronomists, plumbers, accountants, bureaucratic specialists) and the instructors to train them have become vital at this stage of economic and social growth. Shortages and oversupplies of particular types of skills have already become noticeable.

The tendency of the educational system, as in neighboring societies, has been to emphasize literary learning, leading the student ultimately to aspirations for higher education in the liberal professions. In Afghanistan this has meant that while less than one-third of the children go to school and less than 3 per cent of those who do manage to reach the tenth grade, virtually everyone in the secondary schools expects to receive higher education in the nontechnical fields. Consequently, profound manpower problems have begun to emerge. Chronic shortages of industrial workers persist while at the same time there has been an accumulation of university and secondary graduates. A growing number of the best-educated young adults in the society have recently found that there are relatively few opportunities within the small government apparatus for intellectual generalists. Afghanistan has already had to face the potentially dangerous problem of unemployment among the well educated. The coordination of education with manpower needs thus has become vital and is likely to become more difficult to achieve as the schools and the university continue to turn out ever-larger numbers of graduates. Only the most comprehensive coordination of planning, training, personnel recruitment and deployment by all agencies of the government can provide more than partial or interim solutions to the problems involved.

Of nearly comparable importance was the failure of the first two plans to stimulate productive private Afghan or foreign investment. Except for the already established large textile operations controlled by the Bank-i-Milli and some export promotion, private investment had contributed little to development. Yet, if the capacity to produce the wide variety of consumer goods being demanded was to be met from internal resources, it was obvious that private capital had a large role to play. Clothing, food processing, footwear, household articles, spare parts, and luxury goods of simple construction might be produced profitably. Stimulation of private investment for such consumer production was essential for replacing nonproductive imports, training managers and skilled and semi-skilled workers, and broadening the productivity which could be generated from the transportation, energy, and other resources already created. Greater capital investment in internal production could also help absorb part of the excess money supply and thus combat a primary source of inflation. Without a broadening of the base of economic effort through such private activities the achievements of development will have little positive meaning for any but a small minority of Afghans. Prior to the third five-year plan, development had had a marginal effect upon the structure and activities of the total labor force. The largest category of new labor was in construction, but this sector was already declining with the completion of the major infrastructural projects. New small-industry units were therefore needed both to offset impending unemployment and to mobilize the energy and resources which had to be harnessed for a new stage of development.

Mobilization of internal resources for development had also been limited by the inability of the government to develop a tax mechanism capable of capturing capital for productive investment. In several respects fiscal policy and practice have tended to inhibit the pace of development. An extremely small proportion of public revenues is obtained from direct taxes: either from individual or corporate income or from private landholding. Instead, revenue depends heavily upon indirect taxation: import duties, sales of property and government services, fees from licenses and fines, and profits from government commercial operations. A large proportion, as much as 18 per cent, has been acquired from the sale of foreign grain given to the government through the American Food for Peace program. Reliance upon indirect taxes and various types of government services for revenue has permitted most of the economy to be almost untouched by efforts to mobilize internal resources for development. It is estimated that agriculture accounts for at least three-fourths of national income, yet virtually none of this income is subject to taxation, because income taxes rarely apply to agriculture, and land taxation, when enforced, is levied at an extremely low rate. Taxation of livestock has yet to be effectively imposed. These limitations mean that virtually all capital for investment must come from activities related to commerce and foreign trade. While individuals and groups within these sectors enjoy incomes notably larger than typical for agriculture, the effective exemption of crops and herds from taxation leaves few resources available for development investment.

Fiscal dependence largely upon customs duties and government sales and services also tends to confuse and often to interfere with attempts to create greater productivity and a larger volume of exports. Import duties are imposed primarily for the purpose of raising revenue. They account for approximately 25 per cent of government income. Some preferences in customs rates are given to capital goods and other development-oriented imports, but the need for customs revenue tends to inhibit policies which might reduce the volume of consumer imports, e.g., higher tariffs, and thus encourage domestic industry to produce substitutes. Moreover, this reliance upon import duties has resulted in considerable smuggling, especially of consumer goods, thus feeding nonproductive internal demand while at the same time denying revenue to the government.

Export duties are a much less important source of official income, but their imposition tends to discourage efforts to increase the value of exports. More significant has been government manipulation of the proceeds from the sale of export products, most notably karakul skins. Private exporters have been forced to surrender one-half or more of the value of the hard currencies (dollars, pounds sterling, marks) to the government. Consequently, official programs which encourage improved quality in export goods and better grading and packaging in order to insure higher profitability, operate at cross-purposes with foreign exchange regulations which force exporters to surrender a high proportion of their profits to the government.

Other fiscal policies have also discouraged greater productivity and private investment. The bilateral loan agreements with communist-bloc countries which require the supplying of raw wool and cotton, hides, preserved fruits, and vegetable oils for export on a barter basis have forced the Afghan government to take steps to ensure internal purchase of these agricultural products at prices which frequently are unfavorable to producers. While the manipulation of the arbitrary values assigned to these bartered items (the values assigned in the loan agreements have generally not been made public) makes it possible for the government to derive a profit from these bartered commodities, such transactions have tended to discourage agricultural production. Momentary budgetary advantages have thus been gained at the expense of long-term gains in productivity.

The most serious implication of the weaknesses of the taxation and fiscal structure lies in the tendency of the government to depend upon foreign assistance to carry most of the burden of development investment. However necessary this reliance on foreign donors may have been during earlier development phases, such dependence has largely shaped the orientation and performance of the government's fiscal and planning apparatus. As the economy increasingly comes to require sophisticated management, reliance upon foreign aid and foreign advice threatens to become a serious inhibition upon national economic policy. By the late 1960's Afghan development planning and management needed considerable reform. It was necessary to shift the emphasis from foreign-supported construction to increased production based primarily upon indigenous management and capital.

The failure to stimulate greater production was nowhere more obvious than in agriculture. While some progress had been made in some of the larger irrigation schemes and while the relatively small horticultural sector had responded to export opportunities, Afghan agriculture had remained generally stagnant, especially in grain and fiber production. The inputs of capital, water, fertilizers, innovative skills, stronger marketing institutions, and better credit facilities had obviously not combined sufficiently within the setting of the Afghan village to bring about greater total production and larger deliveries to the marketplace. Lacking such a positive response, hopes for broadening and quickening development throughout the economy remained dim. Not only were Afghans dependent upon foreign producers—mostly Indian and Pakistani—for tea and sugar, but increasingly their government had to turn to the Soviet Union and the United States for grain imports. Moreover, the government had grown accustomed to realizing a large proportion of its development revenues from the proceeds from selling this donated grain. Thus the failure of agriculture to meet dietary and industrial needs was being compounded by dependence on these very shortages to generate development capital. The situation did little to inspire confidence for measurable progress in agriculture or the economy as a whole.

These dangers, i.e., inflation, growing foreign debt, imbalances in manpower, immobility of private capital, production shortfalls, and limitations on revenue, combined to force a re-evaluation of Afghan planning in connection with the preparation of the third five-year plan in 1965 and 1966. Assisted by Russian, West German, American, and United Nations advisers, Afghan planning officials attempted to develop a new set of strategies and priorities. While emphasis was placed on completing the unfinished construction projects inherited from the second plan—mostly roads and dams—the primary stress of the third plan was production. Secondary priority was given to expanding health and education services. It was recognized that the era of the large construction project was passing and that an increasing percentage of investment must come from domestic sources both public and private. The primary strategy was to encourage private investment and to improve the government's ability to raise and make effective use of capital.

Integral to the plan was the establishment of such capital-generating agencies as an industrial development bank, an expanded agricultural development bank, and a radical improvement in revenue collection based upon more accurate land and private income records and higher tax rates. Private investment was to be encouraged through legislation which was intended to give domestic and foreign investors incentives to embark upon small and medium-sized industrial and agricultural processing ventures. Incentives included waivers of customs duties and taxes during initial periods of development, technical support from foreign and Afghan government agencies, and easy access to capital through the development banks. These inducements were combined in the Foreign and Domestic Private Investment Law of 1967.

The surveying of industrial prospects carried out by foreign and Afghan experts enabled the mines and industries ministry and the commerce ministry to service new private industrial and commercial operations. The government committed itself to perform more effectively in the fields of fiscal management, project planning and surveying, and the coordination of foreign assistance. It was recognized that in many respects these qualitative changes were even greater departures from past Afghan experience than had been the massive irrigation, transportation, and power projects in the 1950's.

The results of the changes introduced by the third plan were only partially apparent by 1970. Power generation increased from 288 to 320 million kwh. between 1967 and 1970. Extraction of natural gas primarily for export to Russia which had barely begun in 1967 reached 2 billion cubic meters annually in March of 1970. The extension of paved roads to the Persian border and to Mazar-i-Sharif added nearly final stages to the program of linking all major cities with permanent highways. Outside of these important achievements performance has been quite uneven. Fiscal policy aided by good harvests managed to reduce inflation, the consumer price index (with the year 1961–1962 as the base index of 100) dropped from 262 in 1967 to just over 200 in 1970. Modest increases in wheat production were partially responsible for this easing of prices. Output which had hovered near 2,200,000 metric tons since the early 1950's jumped to over 2,350,000 in 1968–1969, an increase of more than 6 per cent which suggests that new agricultural inputs were at last combining for higher productivity.

On the other hand, plans to increase domestic governmental revenues fell far short of their goals. Parliament resisted increases in land revenue rates. Land taxation failed to yield 100,000,000 afghanis—less than 2 per cent of the government's total revenues. Income taxes on both individuals and corporations actually declined after 1966.

The most hopeful areas of development other than in agriculture came from the responses of foreign and domestic investors to invitations to apply for licenses for industrial investment. Under the new investment law more than one hundred applications were filed pledging $35,000,000 in foreign exchange for small and medium-scale ventures. In 1969 more than forty of these were approved and were in early stages of organization or operation. A large share of the applications involved various types of agricultural processing many of which would improve the prospects for greater export earnings. Subsequently, the program suffered setbacks. Allegations were made that some of the new firms were abusing the liberalized import restrictions permitted by the new investment law. The customs authorities moved quickly to halt such practices, but with such effect that many would-be investors appear to have been discouraged, at least in the short run, from continuing their projects. Another difficulty has resulted from the delay of parliament in passing the legislation needed to establish an industrial development bank. Thus much of the credit and technical assistance which was to be available to private investors has been slow to materialize.

Other sectors of the economy demonstrate similarly spotty records. The heaviest industries, coal, cement, and cotton textiles, all declined in output after 1967. Thus, while industrial capacity has been enlarged and some of the tools needed to bring Afghanistan to the state of self-sustaining growth have been installed, recent experience would suggest that considerably more effort will be required before the economy has the strength, depth, and sophistication to develop without outside support. Only a thin layer of expertise and trained leadership, some of it still foreign, controls the levers of the modern sectors of the economy. Continued foreign assistance remains vital for Afghanistan's economic and political growth.

5. Recent Political Development, 1964-1971

With the promulgation of the Constitution of 1964, Afghanistan entered into a new political era. All sectors of the political system have been subject to significant change since then. In facing the dual challenge of democratizing politics while expanding the economy the government has experienced severe problems of institutional adjustment and growth, the emergence of new political forces, changes in the international scene, and the growing need to balance the pace of internal change with cohesion and control.

Institutional change has primarily involved the hammering out of relations between the new parliament and the cabinet. The informal clustering of politicians within parliament is providing a basis for future political dynamics. The directions which such factions might take remains uncertain, but the trends which will determine political competition have begun to grow. Closely related to this process has been the reappearance of a private press. Several private newspapers and journals have attempted to inform and influence public opinion since a private press law was enacted in 1965. Official reaction to the more extreme examples of this new journalism has illustrated the difficulties of broadening participation while maintaining political security.

Relaxation of the pressures and inducements stemming from earlier cold-war competition as it affected foreign assistance to Afghanistan constitutes another major change in the political and economic environment. American involvement in Vietnam and the general loss of support within the U.S. for all foreign assistance programs have combined to cause a sharp drop in American aid. Roughly parallel factors have reduced Russian commitments. Soviet involvement in the Middle East and the spreading of Russian commercial and political connections throughout Asia, partially in response to the challenge presented by Communist China, have reduced Afghanistan's importance in the over-all perspective of Russian foreign policy. As a result, during a period when Afghanistan needs more investment in productive enterprises, external changes have cut the flow of foreign assistance. On the other hand the relaxation of foreign economic rivalry has offered the kingdom greater freedom of action to chart an independent course of political and economic development. In facing economic change and political evolution Afghanistan has entered an era of uncertainty with an enhanced ability to shape its own future.

Political Trends, 1964–1971

Following ratification of the new constitution the interim government under Prime Minister Mohammed Yousuf prepared for the transition to parliamentary government which was to begin after elections scheduled for September, 1965. Its tasks included the drafting of the large number of laws required for the functioning of the new political and judicial processes. Much attention was also given to publicizing the objectives of the constitution and of the steps required to achieve them. The government press made a strenuous effort to explain citizen responsibilities, especially for participation in the elections.

The new press law was enacted during this interim period. It licensed private publications which could use government press facilities. The law stressed the responsibility of private editors for political content. Scope for criticism of the government was limited. Publishers were required to post bond against possible fines for violating the law and the government retained the power to close publications which it considered dangerous to public order. Such actions could be taken without provision for appeal in the courts.

A national election was conducted during the first three weeks of September, 1965. There were no reported incidents of violence or disruption and the election aroused virtually no complaint of government intervention or manipulation of the results. Except for the failure of more than 10 percent of the rural electorate to vote and the even more limited participation of women, the election was judged a success. The representatives elected to the Wolesi Jirga reflected a cross section of all types of Afghan leadership from foreign-educated urban intellectuals to highly conservative mullahs from remote rural districts. They included tribal chiefs or members of their families, private entrepreneurs, left-wing radicals, large and small landholders, poets, and four women—the latter having been elected from city constituencies. Having won election almost entirely on the basis of local issues and local standing, the 215 members did not have commitments to nation-wide political groups (which did not then exist) or to ideological persuasions (which had not yet been publicly articulated). Although a large minority of the members had sat in the previous parliaments or had participated in the 1964 Loya Jirga, few had experience with the parliamentary functions necessary for representing their constituencies or for independent initiation, investigation, or agreement on legislation. Yet while they were untested in these areas of parliamentary activity, almost all of the members were well versed in informal debating tactics learned in their tribal jirgas. Consequently, when it became clear after the first days of the new parliamentary session in October, 1965, that parliament was actually expected to use the powers given it under the constitution, the vocal abilities of the members became considerably more evident than did their capacity for well-organized political action.

The Wolesi Jirga's suspicion of the cabinet coupled with its new-found powers of criticism and review almost immediately created an impasse with the interim government. Prime Minister Yousuf had been selected by the king to organize the first cabinet under the new constitution. He submitted the slate of his prospective ministers to parliament for a vote of confidence. To a large extent its membership coincided with that of the interim cabinet whose tenure would lapse with the new appointments. Opposition to certain individual ministers quickly became a rallying point for a parliamentary challenge to the executive branch. Charges of corruption and incompetence led to demands that the prospective ministers make available complete information on their incomes and property. This demand was accompanied by a rising chorus of complaints and accusations concerning past government actions. Prime Minister Yousuf softened much of this opposition by appealing to the parliament to use the courts to lodge complaints against ministerial wrongdoing. He asked that his cabinet as a whole be approved so that the new era of democracy could begin. A substantial majority of the Wolesi Jirga appeared to accept his argument, but a small group of leftist members persisted in opposition. They called for public demonstrations, thus precipitating the first political crisis of the new era. On October 24, 1965, leftist sympathizers, most of them university students, thronged the parliament building disrupting business and delaying proceedings until the next day.

Parliament voted to hold a closed session on October 25. Crowds of students, some opposed to and some supporting the proposed cabinet, converged on parliament and rioting developed. Police action to break up the mobs was ineffective and by afternoon after considerable damage to nearby public buildings the national army was called in by the interim cabinet (still under Yousuf) to quell the disturbances. Within hours order was restored at the cost of many casualties including, according to official accounts, at least three dead. Thus, even before a cabinet could be installed under the new constitution there had been a traumatic breakdown in the system.

This event was to throw a long shadow over subsequent political developments. It became apparent that a small group of leftist intellectuals, led by Babrak, a Marxist elected to the Wolesi Jirga from Kabul, could foment student demonstrations which could seriously embarrass the government. It also was apparent that the expectations of the new parliament bore little resemblance to what it could accomplish, at least in the opening phases of a new constitutional era. Moreover, the government was stunned by the new sources of violence unleashed by these initial steps toward political change. This greatly increased its caution in accepting or promoting new political initiatives.

The ramifications of the October 25 affair led to the disqualification of the new Yousuf cabinet. Neither the king nor the parliament wished to support leaders held responsible for the catastrophe. The king accepted Yousuf's resignation—given ostensibly for reasons of health— and appointed Mohammed Hashim Maiwandwal as the prime minister designate. Maiwandwal had a civil service background, having served as ambassador to Pakistan, Great Britain, and the United States. He had also been minister of press and information in the interim government. As a political figure he was an almost unknown quantity at the time of his selection.

Maiwandwal moved quickly to win the support of both the parliament and the students. During a visit to the university campus immediately after the riot he assured students that police and government officials who acted brutally would be subject to punishment. Most arrested students and faculty members were released and Maiwandwal conveyed the king's and his own regrets at the bloodshed.

Maiwandwal excluded from his roster of ministers those officials who had been under attack in parliament, and his cabinet was approved without significant opposition shortly thereafter. He remained in control of the government until November, 1967, when he resigned, while seriously ill.

The membership of the Maiwandwal cabinet over-
lapped that of its predecessor. Some younger men who
had not served previously at cabinet level were added in
the development-oriented ministries. Some officials who
had been prominent under Prince Daud were included.
It was characterized as a middle-of-the-road group of administrative and technical managers, few of whom had
an independent political following of their own.

Confronting the new cabinet as it took office was the
hazardous task of operating an untried political system
while establishing a viable strategy for the third five-year
plan which was to begin in the spring of 1967. Virtually
none of the basic laws necessary for orderly conduct of
government had been enacted; the interim cabinet had
been reluctant to use its constitutional power to legislate
by decree fearing that it would have been accused of
pre-empting the powers of the new parliament. The new
cabinet had therefore to push for legislation and for development decisions during a time when the members of
the Wolesi Jirga began to test their potential powers.
Under such circumstances the cabinet was reluctant to
make decisions likely to arouse parliamentary opposition.

For their part the members of parliament worked at
learning their craft including such tasks as the delegation
of legislative responsibilities to committees, the establishment of internal procedures, the cementing of relationships with individual ministries, and the handling of peti-
tions and pressures from private interest groups. One
consequence of the need for both branches to learn their
new roles was the extremely slow pace of decision making
by both the cabinet and the parliament throughout Maiwandwal's administration.

In August, 1966, Maiwandwal described the over-all philosophy and priorities of his government. His announced political and economic goals largely coincided with those laid down in the constitution. He added his own emphasis on steps that would bring a greater measure of economic democracy, principally through more direct government participation in production and possible actions that would bridge the gaps between wealth and poverty. He also stressed the need for balanced development between regions and, therefore, between the major ethnic groups in the society. Generally this statement and other gestures made by the government suggested that it was concerned about the cultural and political shocks which modernization had already begun to bring to the surface of Afghan society. He remained carefully vague about the exact strategy he would employ to bring about development with cohesion.

Partially as a reflection of his own goals and partially to offset the impact of left-wing agitation and antigovernment criticism upon the student community, Maiwandwal put heavy stress upon the rhetoric of social democracy. Yet his cabinet's planning was partially at odds with its slogans favoring greater social control of private wealth. The third plan accepted the proposition that further economic progress clearly required incentives for Afghan and foreign private investment. This inconsistency in socioeconomic policy, the growing rivalry with parliament, the threat of leftist political agitation, and the intrinsic difficulties of economic development induced a policy of caution, sometimes characterized as timidity.

This quality was demonstrated most clearly in the cabinet's handling of the several most prominent issues which emerged in 1966 and 1967. The new press law permitted an indeterminate amount of free expression. During the spring of 1966 the cabinet, with considerable urging by a majority of parliament, silenced private left-wing publications after they appeared to be popularly received in Kabul. Freedom of expression was defined narrowly on the rationale of protecting the new constitutional establishment. Equally as important was the question whether political organizations were to become legal and, if so, under what conditions and with what degrees of freedom. Throughout the Maiwandwal period this issue was debated, but not resolved. The 1967 renewal of war between Israel and the Arab states also proved to have important internal political implications. The government adopted the popular posture of unqualified moral support for the Arab cause—a departure from its careful policy of non-alignment toward virtually all international rivalries which did not directly affect the kingdom. The increasing volatility of internal popular politics undoubtedly contributed to the forcefulness of the official position on the question. It offered an opportunity to harness popular feeling for support of government policies generally.

Another policy of the regime was the relaxation of tension in the dispute over status of Pushtunistan. In contrast to the strident policy followed by the Daud government, both the Yousuf and Maiwandwal cabinets tended to emphasize other political issues. Both maintained a formal posture adamantly in favor of Pushtun independence, but steps were taken to ensure easier trade and diplomatic relations with Pakistan. It appears that the Pushtunistan issue, while still potent among some of the tribes and still sincerely felt by the government, loomed less large in the total spectrum of an enlarged political arena. Under

Daud's tight restrictions on political activity it had been the one major issue about which political expression was encouraged. Since 1963 it has become one among many questions competing for the attention of the politicians and the public.

After a serious illness requiring surgery abroad Maiwandwal submitted his resignation in November, 1967. His successor, Nur Ahmad Etemadi, had served as foreign minister under Maiwandwal and is a member of a family collateral to the royal house. He was appointed without significant parliamentary opposition.

Despite a large number of changes in the cabinet, most of the issues which confronted Maiwandwal persisted. The Etemadi cabinet presided over the orderly election of a new parliament in the fall of 1969. It moved to implement the judicial provisions of the constitution coordinating with the supreme court, which was appointed shortly before the formation of the new cabinet in 1967. The process of jockeying for relative power and defining constitutional and procedural relationships with parliament continued. By the summer of 1970 the cabinet faced increasingly serious parliamentary challenges. Citing the rift between his cabinet and parliament, Etemadi resigned in May, 1971.

The first serious overt opposition to the Etemadi government came during the 1968–1969 school year when university and Kabul secondary students carried out demonstrations which forced the closing of the schools in the capital city for several months. Left-wing students made charges of corruption and official collusion with private capitalists and demanded greater student political rights and the relaxation of academic standards. The government made few concessions and the radical leadership appeared to be effectively isolated by the summer of 1969.

The Etemadi government roughly held its own on questions which it inherited from its predecessor, but it was unable to enlist either the loyalty of the better-educated students or the participation of the majority of the population which continued to pursue its parochial and traditional interests.

This lack of forcefulness also affected the performance of the third plan. Despite encouraging increases in agricultural production and a surprising rise in the foreign exchange earned by tourism, which increased from 8,000 visitors in 1965 to 63,000 in 1969, little was effectively done to mobilize the internal resources needed to maintain expected growth. The government moved slowly to translate growing private investor interest in the Afghan economy into productive projects. Approval of the industrial development bank required three years of parliamentary debate.

While it was capable of avoiding public crises on most of the political issues it inherited, the Etemadi government was unable to mobilize public support for broader and more balanced development. Some of its actions indicated recognition that this is essential. Etemadi attempted to make himself an approachable figure; his demonstration of interest in the living conditions and environment of the rural population culminated in a tour of the most remote provinces of northwest Afghanistan, which had never seen the executive head of a modern government.

With West German help his government moved also to construct grain storage facilities at Kandahar and Herat. Grain elevators had earlier been built at Pul-i-Khumri as well as Kabul. These actions came after distress over grain shortages had reached a peak in 1967 when prices in some cities were twice as high as in others because of regional harvest variations and inadequate freight facilities.

The government also assigned responsibility for the administration of religious affairs to a semiofficial organization, to be known as the Auqaf Administration. It is to function under the supervision of the Ministry of Justice. The organization is to carry out religious policy and provide financial support for the operation of mosques, shrines, and monasteries. It would appear to be a means of centralizing and coordinating government relationships with Afghanistan's traditional religious leaders. It can also monitor and influence their political behavior. Tying these leaders to programs which the government can control and take credit for is a potentially promising strategy for winning religious support for programs which promote sociocultural change. Mullahs and other religious leaders who continue to oppose aspects of modernization, especially the growing role in education being played by women, can increasingly be isolated by exclusion from participation in officially sponsored programs.

The Etemadi cabinet made a serious effort to maintain favorable formal relations with the parliament. It followed the practice begun under Maiwandwal of making cabinet ministers readily available to testify before parliamentary committees. It organized education tours of the ministries for members of parliament. It had also held frequent receptions and other social engagements permitting personal contact between bureaucrats and politicians. While the trend of parliamentary attitudes did not become more favorable to many of the cabinet's policies, there seemed to be little inclination on the part of the cabinet either to bypass or to try to intimidate the legislators. The commitment to the democratization of political institutions remained a major objective, at the cost of political compromises and legislative delays.

Perhaps inevitably the record of the first two governments of the parliamentary era mixes solid accomplishments with considerable failures. Efforts to widen modern sectors of the economy and to ensure that democratic institutions take root remain frustrated in many respects. Two of the most critical examples were the delays in approving an industrial development bank and the failure to enact a law establishing the right to organize political parties. Each is vital for new initiatives in their respective fields. Parliament balked at the bank partially because advantage of its services could initially be taken only by a small number of qualified capitalists. A dispute persisted over the amount of autonomy from government control which the bank's management is to exercise. Opposition from the few parliamentary members who opposed the idea of promoting private investment on ideological grounds appeared to have had much less effect.

The failure to enact a political parties law must be attributed primarily to the caution of the cabinet and perhaps the king. The law has now been passed by both houses of parliament and awaits only the king's signature. It appears that the events which have raised fears about the dangers of uncontrolled political action have raised doubts about the consequences of permitting autonomous political organization. As a result, the informal political alignments and associations essential for the effective functioning of the institutions created in the constitution have been greatly inhibited.

Institutional Relations: The Role of Parliament

The events attending the attempts of parliament to become a potent branch of government since 1965 have yet to be studied in depth. Little is systematically known about the backgrounds of the members, their motives for seeking office, or the crystalization of factions or other groupings within and between the Wolesi and Meshrano jirgas. Accordingly, generalizations concerning the trends and features of parliamentary development must be tentative.

In most respects the new parliament remains politically and institutionally immature. Its role in Afghan politics is still largely undetermined. Its outstanding feature so far has been ability to probe and criticize the performance of the ministries. The constitution limits its involvement in government operations to queries and critiques, although members have discovered that sometimes this prerogative can be used to obstruct and even reverse ministerial actions. Nevertheless, inexperience has forced parliament into a passive posture; the cabinet retains the initiative on almost all matters of major importance for political and economic development.

During its first six years the new parliament has frequently demonstrated its ability to be an effective critic. Its committees have embarrassed officials on several occasions with disclosures of incompetence, corruption, and various forms of favoritism. Members have resisted executive interference with parliamentary business to the extent of formally challenging the motives of the president of the Wolesi Jirga on the ground that he was taking orders from the cabinet (previous to his election he had been a career civil servant). Another instance of parliamentary boldness was the nearly successful attempt in 1970 to remove the minister of information and culture. Unhappy with the coverage of the legislature in the government press, a large minority of the Wolesi Jirga demanded the minister's resignation. The impasse virtually denied him control over the ministry for nearly two months. He survived a no-confidence resolution by fifty-seven votes, thus ending but not resolving a two-headed constitutional crisis. Not only did parliament challenge the constitutional right of an *individual* minister to keep his office against the will of the legislature, but it questioned the right of the press to report parliamentary business.

Important obstacles continue to limit the effectiveness of the Wolesi and Meshrano jirgas. The level of education and political experience possessed by the members contrasts sharply with the qualifications of government officials in the top four or five grades. With perhaps thirty exceptions Wolesi Jirga members possess an average equivalent of little more than an elementary education. They have had virtually no contact with the facets of modern culture which have shaped the outlook of leading government administrators, most of whom have been educated or at least have traveled abroad. Consequently the natural tendency toward institutional rivalry between these two branches of government is softened by the recognition that the officials know a great deal more about contemporary administrative needs and the requirements for effective economic development than do most parliamentarians. Parliament's inclination to probe deeper into government activity and to take its responsibility for legislation with increasing seriousness still is tempered by the awe with which it previously approached the power of the executive. This timidity is declining, but there still remains an imbalance in organization, tradition, and information which allows the cabinet to maintain political leadership.

Few of the instruments available to other national legislatures for influencing, shackling, or reversing executive policy have as yet proved to be effective in Afghanistan. Its parliament has little capacity for research and systematic investigation of public issues or government functions. Instead it has to rely upon interrogation of officials for most of its knowledge. An extension of the formal process of interrogation has been the development of informal connections with government officials who, often for personal reasons, have been willing to leak information to members of parliament. These methods of gathering information have produced a series of widely publicized issues. The experience so far, however, has done relatively little to induce or prepare parliament systematically to develop evidence on which to base legislation.

Parliament's inability to marshal knowledge effectively is partially related to its amorphous political composition. Members have been elected on the basis of their local prominence, often in connection with personal or family influence or power from land, tribal standing, or religious office. Not surprisingly, these primarily traditional qualities of distinction have come to play an important part in the forming of affiliations within the parliament itself. There is a general feeling among most rural members which could be described as conservative. The majority of the members owe their positions to the existing socio-economic and cultural structure of Afghan life, but this orientation has not been the source of effective group identity or organized political activity. While a majority of the members may join together in opposition to some cabinet proposal which threatens them, e.g., land reform, higher land or income taxes, or the authorization of labor unions, these actions have not resulted in ideological unity. In fact, during its short history the new parliament has been unable to organize on the basis of opinion or ideology, Polarities caused by differing political motives have developed, but two factors have prevented stable political groupings: the failure to establish a legal basis for political organization and the constitutional prohibition of overlapping membership between parliament and the cabinet. Despite outspoken criticism of the cabinet, parliament has not been able to devise positive proposals of its own or to provide the foundation for a potential alternative government. Instead, the limitations upon their experience and organization have tended to force parliamentarians into a relationship with the executive which is marked by continual friction and limited legislative results.

Nevertheless, experience is giving the parliament a growing sense of competence and separate identity. It has learned the use of weapons which reduce corruption and bureaucratic arrogance, but it has yet to develop the capacity to take the initiative in issues vital to Afghanistan's political and economic growth. Without an opportunity for further institutional development, it could become mired in an over-long political adolescence during which it would continue to debate and defer important legislation introduced by the cabinet, but would make few positive contributions to the kingdom's political evolution.

Delays in the Formation of Other Political Institutions

The failure to legalize political parties has prevented development of political organizations outside of official institutions formally created by the constitution. Without political parties the evolving system has been unable to sort out political leadership into categories which reach beyond those which have been traditional. Political campaigns at the national level must necessarily be largely artificial exercises when applied to most of the rural constituencies which control 90 per cent of the parliamentary seats. Party organization based upon programmatic and ideological differences would tend to force the issues of modern government and development into dialogues between rival candidates. Without parties elections must turn on questions of reputation or claims of influence within the bureaucracy. These may be relevant as well as persistent factors in the electoral process, but they cannot be expected to stimulate much interest among most citizens nor can they produce effective parliamentary coalitions on issues pertinent to modernization. As a spur to the political mobilization of the great majority of Afghans who have yet to participate in the constitutional system, the polarization of the political process would be potent and dangerous. Yet, without an infusion of greater vitality, the institutions established by the constitution may become irrelevant, ultimately to be disregarded.

The lack of legal organizations also fosters the creation of marginal extremist groups whose opposition to the primary objectives of the constitution already induces them to organize outside the law. This tendency applies both to the most intractable religious reactionaries and to the quasi-Marxist groups which are concentrated among university students and recent graduates. With little access to legitimate arenas of politics (leftist representation was limited to four members of the 1965 parliament; these were all defeated in 1969) radicals are forced to function underground. Government-sponsored youth clubs which have been recently established to promote recreational and cultural activity are not likely to solve the problem of hard-core radical activity. The absence of legitimate forms of organization makes the dangers presented by extremist groups all the more difficult for the government to control or observe. The failure to provide legality for active forms of dissent outside of parliament leaves the door open to political opportunists to make use of extremist groups as bases for assaults upon the government. This temptation could easily appeal to politicians who are not able to gain a following within parliament. Having failed to succeed within the legal system, such politicians would have little alternative but to turn to illegal means to continue their activities.

Local Government Institutions

The beginnings of the slow process of linking provincial and local government to the new constitutional structure at Kabul began in 1966 with the holding of municipal elections in several Afghan cities. There is little formal precedent for representative government at the local level. Varying degrees of participation in tribal and community jirgas have given the rural population, especially the

Pushtuns, informal experience with justice, corporate decisions, and opportunities to provide advice to provincial officials. In some of the larger cities partial self-government has been created through the functions of local chambers of commerce. They have supervised and controlled the commercial activities of their members, providing the government with an instrument of local control.

The intent of the constitution is eventually to establish a full complement of local self-government institutions holding modest executive and legislative powers. Progress toward this goal has been limited to legislation for the election of provincial councils which are to advise governors and their staffs on local matters. The decentralization of legislative and executive functions thus remains almost totally undeveloped. The degree to which local government authorities might eventually become free of the control imposed by the Ministry of Interior will provide a critical index to the degree of political and economic change in Afghanistan. With rare exceptions centrally appointed officials expect to act autocratically and arbitrarily in the provinces. Encouragement of private investment at the beginning of the third plan caused some of the more progressive governors to attempt to stimulate economic and some politically related initiatives on the part of local citizens. The degree to which participation can stimulate new forms of local politics within the many distinct communities in Afghanistan could also affect the pace and depth of economic growth. Thus for many Afghan peasants and nomads the first meaningful sign of cultural change after witnessing the roads, the dams, and the factories may be the recognition that the central government no longer merely wishes to control or pacify them, but has transformed itself into an agency which is willing to share power with them.

The fulfillment of this goal remains in the distant future. Relaxation of arbitrary local administration requires eliminating the government's fears of tribal threats to its authority. Representative local government offers an instrument for winning tribal and other in-group cooperation and greater national loyalty, but caution toward placing new powers in the hands of tribal leaders is justified by recent history.

Press Policy

Caution also continues to prevail in official attitudes toward operation of the private press. Some relaxation has developed since the closing in 1966 of *Khalq,* a Marxist-oriented journal. Most subsequent closings have resulted from economic failure. The literate audience remains extremely small; little income can be generated from subscriptions or advertising. Consequently, the private press and to some extent the government press have few resources with which to develop the journalistic skills and sources of information necessary for creating wide and continuing public interest.

A recent episode involving overenthusiastic praise of Lenin by one private journal suggests that the government is increasing its tolerance of irritating statements in the press. Despite the fact that conservative mullahs protested and publicly demonstrated against the newspaper's use of terms to eulogize Lenin which are normally reserved for the prophet Mohammed, no action was taken to disrupt its publication. In this case the government avoided restricting press freedom, although it could have counted on a generally favorable public reaction if it had done so. Nevertheless, private editors remain on a leash which can be pulled up short at any time. The potential contribution of the Afghan press to the process of democratization through expansion of public interest and participation in the new constitutional system thus continues to be far from adequately realized.

Judicial Reform

The first stages of implementing the constitutional provisions for an independent judiciary which is to establish systematic and secular standards of impartial justice have recently begun. Since 1967 a full complement of nine justices has been appointed to the Afghan supreme court. The high personal quality of the justices is evidence that the government intends to take seriously the creation of a modern and efficient judicial system. As in the case of local self-government, the building process would appear to be an extremely long one. A central judicial secretariat is being organized by the Ministry of Justice, which is also attempting to establish recruiting and training programs for local and provincial judges. The building of a corpus of systematic law which is adequate for the growing complexities of commercial and governmental affairs will be an enormous task.

Zahir Shah and his government accepted large risks in committing themselves to the course of events they started in 1963. The question remains whether they can continue to disperse power while maintaining sufficient checks to retain manageability. It appears that by 1971 the process had produced only modest pressures against the authority of the government. Radical students and mullahs and a few intemperate journalists have all been brought to rein with little expenditure of force. The more powerful currents of change being caused by rapid expansion of education and the modern sectors of the economy will inevitably create political pressures which will test severely the saliency of the constitution and the government's will to implement it fully. Within a relatively short time it will probably be impossible to hamstring parliament's considerable potential powers by forbidding it the right to organize on the basis of party affiliations. Private interests reflecting a variety of ideologies adapted largely from foreign sources will necessarily mature during the next generation. Either they will obtain instruments for adequate organization, representation, and participation in the political process or their strength and frustration will threaten to break the resistance of a government which is too cautious to respond. Recent years have seen only the first phase of the effort to transform narrowly based autocratic control into representational democracy with open public institutions and guarantees of civil liberty.

The Unresolved Question of National Unity

Relatively little overt official attention has been paid to the threats to political unity which might arise from the eventual political mobilization of Afghan minority groups against Pushtun control over government. Cabinet officials have occasionally made reference to the need to make meaningful to the whole population a sense of membership in a single sociocultural community. Some effort has been made to generate a sense of common pride in Afghanistan's composite culture, but the assertion of Aryan descent which is used by Afghan historians to link together the major ethnic groups suggests the difficulty of uncovering devices which give Hazaras, Uzbeks, and Pushtuns a common sense of inheritance.

Recognition that there are potential political dangers in failing to produce a national sense of cohesion was indicated by the restructuring of the old press and information ministry into the Ministry of Information and Culture in 1966. It has undertaken an ambitious program of cultural activities which stress commonality. The revival of handicrafts, folk literature, and folk music, classic devices for arousing national feelings among peoples elsewhere, is being attempted. Recently a serious proposal was made that the ministry establish an academy which would unify the cultural and promotional activities now carried on separately by the Pushtu Academy, the Afghan Historical Society, and the Ariana Encyclopedia.

It remains to be seen whether the inclination of the Pushtun-dominated government to foster a primarily Pushtun-oriented national identity for all Afghans will continue. Previous efforts have included the required learning of Pushtu in the schools, support for research in Pushtu literature, and the enshrining of Pushtu as the national language in article 35 of the 1964 Constitution. The continuation of such a policy may ultimately create opposition from the minorities. Widening political participation makes this question increasingly critical for the future of Afghan unity. An inclusive sense of national identity will be needed to counter ethnic separatism, if political stability is to be successfully combined with representative government.

There is little question that the Pushtuns are capable of continuing their control even with considerable dispersal of power, but there is the danger that as competition for power and wealth enters an increasingly national arena, the traditional parochial blinders which have kept the minorities essentially satisfied with predominance in their own regions will give way to resentment. The manner in which the devolution of political power to provincial and local institutions is to be carried out bears closely upon this question.

The Changing International Position

With the lessening of the tensions behind the competitive foreign assistance which heaped aid upon Afghanistan until the mid-1960's, the kingdom's international position has also entered into a new phase. Reductions in bilateral assistance have been the most obvious symptom. At the same time the prospects have improved for Afghanistan to re-establish, at least partially, its historic crossroads position in international relations and in intra-Asian trade. In this it can expect to have support from many sources. The diplomatic motivations which led to the wide variety of foreign help for Afghanistan still retain enough force to ensure continuing support for its independence and at least a modest level of economic assistance. Each of the major foreign donors continues to have a stake in the kingdom's political and economic viability.

For the U.S., Afghanistan represents the opportunity to help an undeveloped but strategically located nation to progress toward stability and prosperity. In early cold-war perspectives the fact that Afghanistan survives, evolves, and even mildly prospers seems a miracle against the anticipated menace of Soviet penetration and ultimate domination. That such a development has not occurred can therefore be considered a success partially attributable to American diplomacy and assistance. Moreover, Afghanistan's political stability and international neutrality, despite its long Soviet border, allows it to serve in American eyes as an approximation of its role as a nineteenth-century buffer state limiting Russian involvement in South Asia.

While it is increasingly obvious that the Russians have transformed their image of Afghanistan from an obstacle into a bridge for commercial and political contact with Pakistan and India, Russian willingness to accept the independence of Afghanistan and other South Asian states has demonstrated that they tolerate regional nationalism. In place of domination the Russians have been satisfied with alliances based upon reciprocity of interests. This development may be less favorable than the U.S. might have wanted, but it puts the Russians in a difficult position from which to gain political control of these countries through internal penetration and/or revolution. Russian friendship with noncommunist regimes necessarily requires limitations upon their support of domestic Marxist political organizations. Thus the Americans find that although they have been outaided in Afghanistan, the original competition has been partially transformed into a tacit partnership. This understanding reflects an equilibrium of forces playing upon the kingdom which both sides can accept.

For the Soviet Union, the Afghan experience has been expensive, although much of the outlay is to be repaid in agricultural products and natural gas. Probably most important to the Russians have been the political profits gained by treating Afghanistan with generosity and careful respect. Friendly relations and assistance have demonstrated to the rest of the Muslim world, especially to Turkey, Iran, and the Arab states, that the Russians are willing to help a Muslim people whom they could easily conquer or exploit. Afghanistan has served as a showcase for Russia's good intentions in her dealings with other Muslim nations. The demonstration has also assisted Soviet efforts to develop closer relations with the nations of South Asia.

Effective development of Afghanistan's highways into all-weather arteries for trade was another objective of Russian policy. While there was alarm over the potential capacity of Russian- and American-built roads to permit a sudden Russian invasion of Pakistan or India, such military designs could have been carried out, even if more slowly, without paved roads. Apart from the advantages to Afghanistan's internal development, the Russian motivation for road construction appears to have been to open up access for trade in the Indian Ocean region. Their recent efforts to develop closer trade and aid relations with Pakistan as well as India, illustrate the importance to them of modern transportation connections across Afghanistan.

The growth of Russian influence in Afghanistan also can serve as a means for outdoing their rivals, the Chinese Communists, in the contest for support in Asia. This motive was probably secondary when Russian aid was first committed to the Afghans in the mid-1950's. At that time there appeared to be no compelling reason for the Russians to wish to prevent Chinese influences in Afghanistan. With the deterioration of relations between these two Marxist powers, competition may have become an increasingly important factor governing Russian policy. They have maintained far greater influence than the Chinese in Afghanistan; by the indexes of money, resident manpower, volume of trade, and the continuity of political commitments the Chinese have been restricted to a minor role.

Another incentive for the Russians lies in the potential value of their creditor position. The Afghan economy and therefore, to some extent, the Afghan diplomatic position, are dependent upon the USSR. However much they try to balance this dependence with assistance from other sources, it still restricts their freedom of action on international questions sensitive to the Russians. This ability to restrain possible Afghan acts of hostility has not required crude or abrupt exercise. Merely the insurance that a neighbor with a long common border will not be inclined to take actions which could upset or interfere with Russian interests is a valuable gain.

More marginal is the benefit of preventing a military deployment in Afghanistan which could threaten the Soviet Union. This permits the Russians to concentrate their conventional military defenses along other stretches of their vast perimeter. The large role which they have played in internal Afghan development virtually ensures that no other major power can use the kingdom as a military base against the Russians. This possibility has been made all the more remote by the Russian monopoly in equipping and training Afghan military forces.

Thus, while they conflict in certain areas of interest, the Russian and American objectives concerning Afghanistan were mutually achieved to the point where both sides appeared ready to scale down their involvement in the late 1960's. Yet each power continues to have a stake in maintaining Afghanistan's neutral role in Asian politics. It can therefore be expected that both of them will maintain their presence, but less obviously in the near future.

Regional Diplomacy

Among Afghanistan's Asian neighbors, relations with Pakistan have been the most painful and most important since the latter became independent in 1947. The overriding issue between the two nations has been Pushtunistan. Animosity reached its peak during the last years of Prince Daud's regime and the dispute has since remained as a less important but still live issue in internal Afghan affairs.

Late in the 1960's political events inside Pakistan made possible a warming of relations. Mohammed Yahya Khan's seizure of power in early 1969 set in motion changes permitting steps toward resolution of the dispute. The Afghans applauded Yahya Khan's decision to re-establish a multiprovince system in West Pakistan as a recognition of the need for Pushtun autonomy east of the Durand Line.

This improvement in relations is of major importance to Afghanistan. It assures that the best route will be open by which Afghan goods can earn the hard currencies of Western Europe and the United States and thus balance her foreign trading relationships between the Soviet and Western blocs. As long as Pushtunistan disrupted relations between the two countries, the transit arrangements which permitted Afghan goods to cross Pakistani territory were always in danger of being upset or delayed. Moreover, hostility had unnaturally restricted the amount of trade between the two countries. Pakistan has purchased far less Afghan fruit than has India, although shipments to India have had at times to be air-freighted across West Pakistan. On the other hand Pakistani textiles and other manufactures have not reached their potential for supplying the Afghan market. The satisfaction of complementary needs becomes more probable with improvements in their relations.

Closer Afghan relations with Pakistan are also an extra dividend for the Russians as recent Russian economic diplomacy toward Pakistan suggests. When the two Islamic countries are friendly enough to have close economic relations, Russian opportunities to develop overland trade across Afghanistan into South Asia are notably improved. The recent Soviet offers to provide industrial and other credits to Pakistan indicate this combination of interests between the three parties.

Largely as a function of her relationship with Pakistan, Afghanistan has generally maintained cordial relations with India. The Indians have thought it worthwhile to court the Afghans as a potential counterweight to West Pakistan whose army is concentrated along its common border with India. This strategy appears never to have been based upon more than a vague possibility, but as long as the Pushtunistan question upset Afghan-Pakistan relations it provided an incentive for Indo-Afghan amiability. The active trade between the two countries has been solid. India takes the largest share of Afghan fruit exports in return for which she supplies sugar, tea, and a variety of consumer goods. The determination of the Indians to continue friendly relations is suggested by the offer made in 1970 to help Afghanistan develop a direct route to the Arabian Sea by means of an all-weather road through the Iranian province of Kirman.

This latter proposal also indicates that the Iranians are

willing to develop closer relations with the Afghans. In the twentieth century, except for a brief period during Amanullah's reign, the two nations have either had inactive or passively hostile relations, despite their common possession of Persian culture. Although they have a long common border, it has served more as a source of disagreement, particularly over territory in the Seistan region, and as a buffer because the regions on either side of it are undeveloped and offer poor communications. Consequently there has been little trade apart from the movement of nomads and their herds whose transactions are officially looked upon as smuggling.

The sectarian division between Shia and Sunna continues to be a barrier to closer relations. It is also possible that the head start which Iran gained in development—partly through beginning earlier than Afghanistan but largely because of the exploitation of her oil reserves—have helped to keep relations distant. It is possible that the common cultural heritage has given rise to a sense of rivalry. Despite its greater wealth Iran has shown little inclination to offer significant assistance to Afghanistan, and in turn the Afghans have not looked to Iran as a source or model for modernization.

Connections which have developed between the two royal families may presage improved relations between the two nations. Since the shah of Iran established firm control over his own kingdom in the 1950's there has been a tendency for the younger members of the royal families to exchange visits. The shah participated as mediator in the negotiations which reopened the Afghan-Pakistan border in 1963.

The focus of Afghan international concerns shifted

considerably with the government's public reaction to the events surrounding the Arab-Israeli war of June, 1967. In most respects Afghanistan had been remote from Arab politics. The two previous wars in the Middle East had little impact on Afghan thinking or official government policy. It is perhaps symptomatic of the changes in the political system in the 1960's that much greater identity with the Arab cause was expressed in 1967. The traditional interest in the fate of brother Muslim communities has been revitalized with the opening of opportunities for public debate. The government did not wish to allow private spokesmen, particularly the more conservative mullahs who are opposed to the government's policies on other matters, to monopolize the mobilization of public opinion against Israel. A gesture of support for the Arab combatants in the form of medical assistance was made with considerable publicity. It was largely financed through private donations. The episode suggests that emotional issues affecting the international Islamic community can have an effect upon the evolving process of Afghan politics.

The Growing Orientation toward International and Regional Associations

Until its brief association with the League of Nations in the 1930's Afghanistan had had little experience with international organizations. Until the 1960's the kingdom's most immediate interests were tied to bilateral relations. A charter member of the United Nations, Afghanistan's neutralism restrained her from playing an active role in its affairs especially after no satisfaction was obtained from the U.N. on Pushtunistan. As the variety of foreign assistance and the reach of her foreign trade contacts has grown, Afghanistan has taken greater interest in the U.N. and related international agencies.

In addition to having the honor of its U.N. representative, Abdur Rahman Pazhwak, serve as president of the General Assembly in 1966–1967, Afghanistan has moved toward greater participation in the activities of U.N. development and assistance agencies operating in Asia. Afghanistan is represented on ECAFE (Economic Commission for Asia and the Far East) and is also a charter member of the Asian Development Bank. Afghanistan has also participated actively in the U.N. Commission for Trade and Development (UNCTAD) which has pitted the less-developed nations against the great industrial states on questions of international trade policy. Increasing interest has developed in such trading associations as GATT (General Agreement on Tariffs and Trade), a clearinghouse for the regulation of international trade and in establishing relations with the European Common Market as a means of expanding hard currency earnings. These associations signify that the Afghans are a long way from the days of British tutelage in foreign affairs. The most casual observation of commercial and political activities in Kabul provides convincing evidence that Afghanistan has entered into the international community, although her role there has remained largely undefined.

Conclusion: The Continuing Quest for Democracy, Prosperity, and Independence

Despite the considerable achievements of installing constitutional government, moving toward greater economic sophistication, and maintaining political independence, Afghanistan has yet to devise the formulas needed to cement and add to these accomplishments. Every step of progress has yielded problems which challenge the country's inexperience and institutional unpreparedness. Perhaps the most important of these is the need to reach a decision on the degree to which the traditional roots of Afghan society can be blended with the attractions and imperatives of modern, largely western culture.

The continuing adolescence of Afghanistan's political and governmental system is apparent in the limited results so far achieved in implementing the new constitution, the failure to produce the goods and services which an increasing number of citizens demand, or in freeing its internal affairs from the influences of foreign governments. Afghanistan as an evolving nation thus remains in an early stage of development. Accordingly, it can be anticipated that further political development will subject its system to pressures against which it is vulnerable. The following themes would appear to be especially significant for the immediate future.

ACCUMULATION OF EXPERIENCE

Perhaps the most obvious characteristic of contemporary Afghan government is its inexperience in nearly every modern internal function. With the possible exception of public order, every government activity is the subject of experimentation regarding function, objectives, and priorities. Government agencies are obliged to discover and train staff and to organize resources for purposes which a few years before were not considered essential to the survival of the government or to the needs of the people. This lack of experience contributes to an attitude of caution and has produced innumerable delays in the execution of what often appear to foreign observers to be simple administrative tasks. Afghan officials tend to work slowly because they often are confused by what is expected from them and are uncertain of responsibilities which require the employment of unfamiliar methods. This lack of confidence has resulted in much spreading and sharing of responsibility. Delays have also been caused by sheer lack of information necessary for decision making and ignorance of applicable administrative or technical procedures. Thus, only in the middle 1960's was sufficient reliable statistical information beginning to become available for economic planners to work with data on income, productivity, money supply, revenues, foreign trade, commodity supplies, and physical resources. Basic premises regarding total population and its sex and age components, size of the labor force, and national income still must rely upon estimates with wide margins for error. Consequently, in most areas where innovation is a major concern, Afghan politicians and administrators have been forced to grope in the dark.

THE IMPORTANCE OF QUALITY

With the completion of most infrastructural needs the challenges of further economic and institutional progress in Afghanistan are far more qualitative than quantitative in nature. Future progress will be increasingly dependent upon how effectively facilities and resources are used, not upon the magnitude of road mileage, kilowatt hours, irrigation canals, or mineral deposits. Qualitative improvements depend primarily upon human and institutional mobilization. A point has been reached in development where the quality of decision making, managerial performance, coordination between agencies, degree of public support, and level of technical skills must be linked in ways which are mutually reinforcing. Invariably, progress of this type is fragile and subject to imbalance and frustration. Accordingly, the measurement of either political or economic progress in the near future will be more difficult than heretofore, and the results are likely to be less obviously satisfying to the Afghans themselves.

BALANCED INSTITUTIONAL CHANGE

The tentative attempts of the leadership in the cabinet, parliament, courts, and private business to find, expand, and perfect their roles in the evolving system indicates the delicacy of balance which must be maintained if political and economic development are to take place without disruption. Considerable danger still attends the parallel growth of legislative and executive functions. Sudden shifts in power between them remain highly likely. Over-reaction or obstruction by one branch against the other could yet upset the basis for further growth. While success in Afghanistan's democratic experiment is far from assured, the results of the first six years suggest that the executive branch which retains most political initiatives is still committed to a progressive sharing of power.

INTERNAL POLITICO-CULTURAL POLARITIES

Special dangers arise from two related aspects of current political development: the paradox of conservative, rural forces gaining control of the widened powers given parliament, at the expense of the urban middle class intelligentsia which was primarily responsible for designing the constitution; and the widening of the gap between the relatively modern institutions in the towns and the persistence of traditional norms and behavior in the countryside.

Recent attempts by some students and left-wing groups to influence political events and government policy are symptomatic of the irony that the democratic and primarily liberal constitution-embodied goals of the urban, educated minority are subject to the will of a parliament controlled by rural conservatives who neither understand nor sympathize with such goals. The tensions which have resulted are both creative and dangerous. The modern intelligentsia which largely overlaps the cabinet and upper levels of the bureaucracy, must learn to cope with the fact that the institutions created by the constitution are largely controlled by men who accept them passively, at best. It is possible that with gradual accumulation of experience, confidence, and acceptance of the game, a growing proportion of the conservatives in parliament may become committed to the goals of the system. Their participation, however, may cause some of the weight given the human rights defined in the constitution to be lost. It is also possible that the frustrations of the educated elite may produce a confrontation either within parliament or between parliament and the ministries which will bring about a paralysis or complete breakdown of authority. The path leading to a broad consensus on political goals and processes appears to lead far into the future, primarily because the rivalry between modernists and conservatives is likely to continue indefinitely, fueled by new issues and by new forms of competition for power.

The gap between urban and rural development has

been aggravated in the course of Afghanistan's political and economic development. A few cities have monopolized the resources required for both types of innovation. It is possible that further parliamentary political development and the gradual spread of provincial and local governmental autonomy will help to reverse this trend, but most indicators suggest that the contrasts between urban and rural opportunities will continue to widen. This phenomenon could severely disrupt Afghanistan's future development. Current symptoms of this process include the growing aversion of educated Afghans to living or serving outside of the major cities or even, in many cases, away from Kabul itself. The concentration of the best schools, hospitals, cultural and recreational facilities, and politico-economic opportunities at the capital and to a far lesser degree at the major provincial cities, has stimulated urban migration which further aggravates the imbalances in talent and experience. The contrast between urban modernism and rural conservatism can only become sharper, if the great majority of the brightest and best-educated village youths migrate from the farms and do not return. This problem is far from unique to Afghanistan. Its precise effect upon the evolution of the political and economic systems is difficult to project, but it can be expected to encourage extreme obscurantism and xenophobic demands by rural leaders who wish to capitalize upon agrarian resentments against urban monopolization of economic and political benefits. The government has given attention to this question especially since the mid-1960's. Some agencies now require that officials, usually at early stages of their careers, must serve in district or provincial posts and be provided housing and salary incentives to compensate for rural hardships. Such policies can do little to check the widening of the gap. As education becomes available to a growing proportion of the population and economic progress makes occupational and spatial mobility easier, the movement from country to city is likely to accelerate and to create increasingly difficult problems for both sectors.

THE ATTRACTIONS OF FOREIGN MODELS

Afghan attempts to accelerate the development of their country are more than marginally influenced by competing foreign models and experiences. Afghans who have received the advanced training which allows them to take upper administrative or technical positions often reflect the attitudes of the foreign countries where they have gone for advanced study. Furthermore their career interests often become associated with the assistance programs of the same nations. Since several major foreign powers and the U.N. have contributed to this type of polarity, no one foreign influence has become predominant, but the phenomenon of compartmentalism on the basis of foreign training and experience is a potentially divisive factor. This problem is related to the need for facility in a foreign (usually European) language. Thus, an Afghan engineer trained in Russia and another with comparable American training are likely to find that not only their technical skills differ, but that each cannot easily share his range of foreign cultural experience with the other. In Afghan ministries where four or five different foreign donors are offering training abroad to a group of Afghan officials, functional coordination and the setting of common goals by the Afghans themselves has been complicated by the varying foreign viewpoints, practices, and standards which they have separately acquired.

These many-sided pulls of foreign influence require counteraction by the Afghan determination to make goals, strategies, and techniques serve needs which are unique to Afghanistan. The competing models presented by foreigners raise questions about the alternatives available to the kingdom. In this context such obvious ideological issues as public versus private control of the economy or the suitability of single, double, multiple, or nonparty political systems may not be significant. No major sector of the economy or government can achieve its maximum contribution to development through simple imitation of some impressive foreign system. Unique sectoral and regional conditions apply to Afghan agriculture, animal husbandry, and commerce. Indigenous practices need not be less efficient in their own environment than foreign techniques which have proved themselves elsewhere. Adaptations peculiar to the country will be required of most institutional or technical importations, if they are to be viable. They must respond to indigenous aspirations and apply to indigenous needs. Consequently, the effort to overcome the seductive attractions of foreign technical and economic examples must be expanded if Afghans are to develop sufficient clarity of focus on what they want and how they are to achieve it.

RESPONSES TO SPECIAL PROBLEMS AND OPPORTUNITIES

Recent events in Afghanistan have demonstrated that the emergence of particular problems or opportunities will continue to have great weight on the direction, pace, and degree of success of efforts at development. Thus, sudden crises over the role and activities of the students and the private press have had a great deal to do with the general political atmosphere in which the government has operated. The timing and magnitude of these and similar issues will continue to present awkward situations which can affect the government's ability to achieve further political or economic growth. There are also opportunities, especially in economic development, which could have profound effects upon Afghan society. The recent discoveries of large reserves of natural gas and of high grade iron ore make heavy industry at least theoretically possible. Surveys of energy, transportation, and market requirements do not yet give a clear picture of the importance of these discoveries. The exporting of natural gas, however, has already had a major bearing on economic relations with the Soviet Union. The development of an iron and perhaps a steel industry would bring revolutionary changes to Afghanistan's labor force, foreign trade, and transportation system. If it were to be the size necessary to be profitable, such an industry would also create profound economic, social, and probably, political changes. However, unless entirely new factors soon enter the Afghan picture it seems likely that transformations of this magnitude remain far in the future.

THE CONTINUING ROLE OF THE MONARCHY

Although the constitution discourages the king's active participation in politics, and excludes his family from important offices, the political potency of the crown cannot be overlooked. The character of the king and his relationships with close relatives have been central to Afghan politics for over two centuries, including the pe-

riod of Musahiban rule. Royal passivity is not to be taken
for granted. In fact, the degree to which Zahir Shah was directly involved in the policies of the Yousuf, Maiwandwal,
and Etemadi cabinets, while not precisely known, is believed to have been considerable. The king has the personal qualities and the institutional nexus with all
important elements in the political system to dominate
the cabinet and the parliament. Thus, Afghanistan's political future still remains largely at the disposal of the
monarch. While he would find it extremely difficult to
turn back the clock, he could re-establish arbitrary rule
which would disregard the intent, if not the letter of the
constitution. Zahir Shah has taken the experiment begun
in 1964 seriously, but he or his successors may find it
necessary to assume direct control of government. The
persisting close personal relationship between the king
and his senior military officers suggests that he wishes
to keep this option viable. Even without his assuming
an overt role, Afghan politicians value the king's support
and the most politically sensitive are aware that personal
and generational divisions within the royal family itself
still have the capacity to shape or divert the political
process.

Despite the many imponderables and difficulties obstruct-
ing development and democratization in Afghanistan,
recent events demonstrate that Afghan leadership is committed to greater economic and social opportunity for all
sectors of the population. Achievement of these goals will
require extraordinary balance and resilience in political
stewardship. The contemporary world is full of examples
of nations whose imbalance in politicoeconomic develop-

ment has produced chaos or dictatorship on the one hand or economic stagnation or socioeconomic polarization on the other. The Daud era demonstrated the limitations of an exclusive concern with economic development at the expense of the broadening of political participation. Overly great concern at present with parliamentary-executive relations at the expense of effective economic management could prove to be equally dangerous. Having broadened the political system dramatically in the middle 1960's the Afghan government and people must achieve increasingly higher levels of mutual cooperation, understanding, and cohesion if they are to reach most of their goals. Afghanistan's recent history shows how difficult such a feat will be, but it also suggests that the Afghans are capable of it.

Sources and Bibliography

Students of Afghanistan face difficulties in locating resources, but not because published or archival material is scarce. Wilber lists 1,600 titles in his most recent (1968) bibliography and T. I. Kukhtina's Bibliography (*Bibliografia Afganistana Literatura na russkom iazyke* [Moscow, 1965]), covering publications in Russian only, has 5,680 entries. Much of the difficulty lies in the scattering of material among collections and publications in Asia, Europe, and North America. No archival or library collection outside of Afghanistan holds more than fragments of the total literature, and the organization of materials within Afghanistan is rudimentary. The scattering of sources is closely correlated with the diversity of languages required for Afghan studies. Persian, Pushtu, French, Russian, German, and English are the most useful, but cultural materials and antiquities can demand the use of Italian, Japanese, Danish, Swedish, and Czech, and much of the historical literature is accessible only through Arabic, Urdu, and Turkish.

Study is further hindered by an acute topical imbalance in the published literature and available, useable data. Travel accounts of widely varying value are plentiful. History, literature, and language have received most of the scholarly attention. Except for the Pushtun tribes little effective inquiry was made into Afghan institutions, social, religious, economic, political, or ethnic-regional, prior to the Second World War.

Consequently, there is as yet little evidence on features of agriculture, pastoralism, crafts, internal trade, land tenure, religious particularism, marriage, interethnic relations, law enforcement, child-rearing practices—the subjects which come closest to defining the variety and content of Afghan life.

Much of the historical literature in English concerns Afghanistan as an element in the defense of imperial India against anticipated Russian threats. Corresponding interests dominate Russian works. With such exceptions as Charles Masson (*Narrative of Various Journeys in Baloochistan, Afghanistan, the Punjab and Kalat* [London, 1842]), Sir Alexander Burnes (*Cabool* [London, 1842]), Munshi Mohan Lal (*Life of the Amir Dost Mohammed Khan of Kabul* [London, 1846]), few accounts of Afghanistan before 1900 were based upon prolonged, direct contact by foreigners. In fact, only during the past twenty years have favorable opportunities developed for the collection of sociocultural data on a systematic basis either through field studies or information gathering by Afghan government agencies and their foreign associates. Thus, despite the considerable literature which has been devoted to it, Afghanistan remains largely unknown; rigorous scholarship on the most vital aspects of its life is at an early stage and depends largely upon the collaboration established between Afghan and foreign scholars.

The most valuable publicly accessible collection in Afghanistan is maintained by the Ministry of Information and Culture at the Kabul Public Library. It is strongest on history—largely in European languages—and is the repository for domestic publications in Persian and Pushtu. Files of newspapers, government publications, laws, and treaties are kept, but their storage is unorganized and the documentary material is poorly cataloged. The Kabul University Library is much easier to use, but has fewer domestic documents and publications. Specialized current materials on the economy can be found at the libraries of the Ministry of Planning and the

Bank-i-Milli. The Court Library which is a major interest of Zahir Shah is reputed to be one of the most complete and well organized on Afghanistan, but admittance is restricted.

For many areas of inquiry the U.S. Library of Congress maintains an adequate collection on Afghanistan. It holds as many as 500 titles and most current or recent periodicals and metropolitan newspapers published by the Afghan government. The U.S. Agency for International Development keeps in Washington, D.C., an extensive collection of reports, surveys, and other materials prepared by its own representatives and foreign and international agencies concerned with Afghanistan over the past twenty years. Agriculture, foreign trade, public administration, and education are most strongly represented. Such materials can be obtained from the agency under the provisions of the U.S. Public Information Act of 1967.

No American university has as yet a comprehensive collection on Afghanistan.

The most valuable archival sources for Afghanistan's diplomatic history and foreign trade relations are the Indian National Archives at Delhi and the Commonwealth Relations Office in London. The American National Archives at Washington and those of the German Foreign Office at Bonn have materials essential for the study of German (and Italian) involvement in Afghanistan from the 1920's through the Second World War.

American students will find Donald N. Wilber (*Annotated Bibliography of Afghanistan,* 3rd ed. [New Haven: Human Relations Area Files Press, 1968]) to be the most effective guide to substantial publications on the country. George Grassmuck et al. (*Afghanistan: Some New Approaches* [Ann Arbor: Center for Near Eastern and North African Studies, U. of Michigan, 1969]) extends the coverage of the Wilber bibliography. It also provides a bibliography of recent Russian publications and a list of materials available from USAID.

Both of these bibliographies have proved to be invaluable in the preparation of the references presented here.

Public information and current and useful nonclassified materials can be obtained from the embassies of Afghanistan in London and Washington and from the U.S. Department of State and its embassy in Kabul. Contemporary developments can most quickly and easily be followed by consulting the three major metropolitan Kabul newspapers: Kabul *Times* (English), *Anis* (mostly Persian, some Pushtu), and *Islah* (mostly Pushtu, some Persian). The official monthly magazine, *Afghanistan*, publishes articles on history, culture, and contemporary developments, many of which have research value.

No discussion of materials on Afghanistan would be complete without a reference to the series of reports prepared for the American University Field Service by Louis Dupree. Beginning in 1959, Dupree has provided a potpourri of information and informed analysis on Afghan politics, foreign policy, economic development, social change, and ethnic minorities which is unique in its scope, reliability, and timeliness. To indicate the value of his AUFS reports they are listed here instead of in the chapter bibliographies.

Dupree, Louis. *American Universities Field Service Reports on Afghanistan.*

   Vol. 3 (1959): no. 2, "The Burqa Comes off"; no. 3, "An Informal Talk with Prime Minister Daud."

   Vol. 4 (1960): nos. 3–5, "Afghanistan's Big Gamble," pts. I–III; no. 6, "The Mountains Go to Mohammad Zahir: Observations on Afghanistan's Reactions to Visits from Nixon, Bulganin and Khrushchev, Eisenhower, and Khrushchev"; no. 7, "The Bamboo Curtain in Kabul: An American Finds Communications with the Chinese Embassy Closed to Him"; no. 8, "A Note on Afghanistan"; no. 9, "American Private Enterprise in Afghanistan."

   Vol. 5 (1961): nos. 2–4, " 'Pushtunistan': The Problem and Its Larger Implications," pts. I–III.

Vol. 6 (1962): no. 1, "India's Stake in Afghan-Pakistan Relations"; no. 3, "The Indian Merchants in Kabul"; no. 5, "Landlocked Images."

Vol. 7 (1963): no. 1, "Afghanistan's Slow March to Democracy"; no. 2, "The Afghans Honor a Muslim Saint"; nos. 3–4, "A Suggested Pakistan-Afghanistan-Iran Federation," pts. I–II; no. 5, "The Green and the Black" (social and economic aspects of a coal mine in Afghanistan); no. 7, "The Decade of Daoud Ends"; no. 9, "An Informal Talk with King Mohammad Zahir of Afghanistan."

Vol. 8 (1964): no. 1, "Mahmud Tarzi: Forgotten Nationalist"; no. 4, "The Peace Corps in Afghanistan."

Vol. 9 (1965): nos. 1–4, 10, "Constitutional Development and Cultural Change," pts. I–IV, VIII.

Vol. 10 (1966): no. 1, "Ethnographic Puzzle"; no. 2, "Kabul Gets a Supermarket"; no. 4, "Afghanistan: 1966"; nos. 9–10, "Aq Kupruk: A Town in North Afghanistan," pts. I–II; no. 11, "The Chinese Touch Base and Strike Out."

Vol. 12 (1968): no. 2, "A Kabul Supermarket Revisited"; nos. 4–7, "Afghanistan, 1968," pts. I–IV.

Vol. 14 (1970): no. 1, "Sports and Games in Afghanistan"; nos. 3–4, 6, "Free Enterprise in Afghanistan," pts. I–III; no. 5, "The 1969 Student Demonstrations in Kabul"; no. 7, "Population Dynamics in Afghanistan."

Chapter 1. Physical and Social Setting

Data on geographical and climate features and agricultural resources have been taken from Wilber (1962), the Kabul *Times Annual* (1967), U.S. Department of State, *Background Notes on Afghanistan* (1968), Paul (1970), and the Afghanistan Ministry of Planning, *Survey of Progress* (1969). The observations on location and communications were influenced by Gregorian (1969) and Stewart (1961). Many authorities have made estimates of the Afghan population.

Wilber's arguments would place the total considerably below the more than 15 million claimed by the government. Recent population growth, which can be presumed to be a result of improved controls over endemic diseases, suggests a figure perhaps 2 million above Wilber's ten-year-old computation.

Linguistic, ethnic, and social data were drawn from Wilber (1962), the Kabul *Times Annual* (1967), Gregorian (1969), Fletcher (1965), Schurmann (1961), Spain (1963), and Ferdinand (1959). Throughout the chapter and especially with regard to geographical, economic, and regional-ethnic patterns, personal travel and observation influenced emphasis and treatment. The following titles are commended for further study.

GEOGRAPHY

Cressey, George B. *Crossroads: Land and Life in Southwest Asia.* Chicago: J. B. Lippincott, 1960. Pp. 136–39, 545–582.

Gregorian, Vartan. *The Emergence of Modern Afghanistan: Politics of Reform and Modernization, 1880–1946.* Palo Alto: Stanford University Press, 1969.

Humlum, Johannes. *La geographie de l'Afghanistan.* Copenhagen: Gyldendal, 1959. The most definitive study completed prior to recent aerial mapping.

Kabul *Times Annual, 1967.* Nour M. Rahimi, ed. Kabul: Kabul Times Publishing Agency, 1967. Pp. 86–152. Includes fact-filled chapters on climate, topography, and provincial statistics.

Michel, Aloys. "Johannes Humlum, *La geographie de l'Afghanistan,*" review article, *Economic Geography,* 36, no. 4 (1960), 355–368.

Paul, Arthur. "Economic Survey of Afghanistan." In *Middle East and Australasia.* London: Europa Publications, 1970. Pp. 129–134.

Puliarkin, V. A. *Afganistan: Ekonomicheskaia geografiia* (Afghanistan: Economic Geography). Moscow: Mysl, 1964.

Reisner, Igor Mikhailovich. *Afganistan S Kartami i skhemami* (Afghanistan with Maps and Charts). 2d ed. Moscow: Konnunisticheskaia Akademiia; Institut Mirovogo Khazaistva i Mirovoi Politiki; Kolonial 'naia Seriia, 1939.

Stewart, Ruth W. "Caravan Trade in Asia with Special Reference to Afghanistan." Mimeographed. Kabul: U.S. Operations Mission, 1961.

U. S. Department of State. *Background Notes on Afghanistan, June 1968.* Washington: Government Printing Office, 1968.

Wilber, Donald N., ed. *Afghanistan.* New Haven: Human Relations Area Files, 1962.

SOCIAL AND CULTURAL INSTITUTIONS

Ali, Mohammad. *Manners and Customs of the Afghans.* Lahore: Punjab Educational Press, 1958.

Aslanov, M. G. et al. "Ethnography of Afghanistan." Mark and Greta Slobin, trans. In George Grassmuck et al., *Afghanistan: Some New Approaches.* Ann Arbor: Center for Near Eastern and North African Studies, U. of Michigan, 1969. Pp. 11–80.

Bacon, Elizabeth. "An Inquiry into the History of the Hazara Mongols of Afghanistan," *Southwest Journal of Anthropology,* 7 (1951), 230–247.

———. "The Hazara Mongols of Afghanistan: A Study in Social Organization." Unpublished Ph.D. dissertation, University of California, Northern Section, 1951.

Debets, G. F. "Antropologicheskie issledovaniia a v Afganistan" (Anthropological Studies in Afghanistan), *Sovetskaia Etnografia,* no. 4 (1967), pp. 75–93.

Elphinstone, Mountstuart. *An Account of the Kingdom of Caubul and its Dependencies in Persia, Tartary, and India: Comprising a View of the Afghaun Nation, and a History of the Dooraunee Monarchy.* London: Longman, Hurst, and John Murray, 1815. A classic and still largely relevant account of Afghan society and politics.

Farhadi, A. G. Ravan. "Languages (in Afghanistan)." *Kabul Times Annual, 1967,* pp. 83–85.

Ferdinand, Klaus. "Preliminary Notes on Hazara Culture."

Det Kongelige Danske Videnskaberres Selskab. Historisk-filosofiske Meddelelser, B.d. 37. No. 5. Copenhagen: Ejnar Munksgaard, 1959.

———. "Nomad Expansion and Commerce in Central Afghanistan: A Sketch of Some Modern Trends," *Folk*, 4 (1962), 123–159.

Fletcher, Arnold. *Afghanistan: Highway of Conquest*. Ithaca: Cornell University Press, 1965.

Furon, Raymond. *L'Afghanistan*. Paris: Albert Blanchard, 1926.

Hackin, Ria and Ahmad Ali Kohzad. *Legendes et Coutumes Afghanes*. Paris: Presses Universitaires de France, 1953.

Jenkins, Robin. *Dust on the Paw*. New York: G.P. Putnam's Sons, 1961.

———. *Some Kind of Grace*. London: MacDonald, 1960. Two novels on life in Kabul.

Jentsch, C. "Typen der Afrarlandschaft im Zentralen und Oestlichen Afghanistan." *Arbeiten aus dem Geographischen Institut*, Vol. X. University of the Saar, 1966. Pp. 23–68.

Kennedy, T. F. *Afghanistan Village*. The World's Villages, No. 4. London: Longman's, 1967.

Malyshev, Iu. I. "Some Basic Features of the Socio-Economic Structure of Afghanistan," *Izv. AN Kaz. SSR ser. obshchestv, nauk*, 3, no. 2 (1965), 68–79.

Mandelshtam, A. M. *Kochevniki na puti v Indiiu* (Nomads on the Route to India). Moscow-Leningrad: Nauka, 1966.

Robertson, George S. *The Kafirs of the Hindu Kush*. London: Lawrence and Bullen, 1896. The most complete source on pre-Islamic Nuristan.

Schurmann, H. F. *The Mongols of Afghanistan*. The Hague: Mouton, 1961. While primarily concerned with Mongol remnants (not Hazaras) it presents valuable observations on all major Afghan ethnic-linguistic groups.

Shah, Sirdar Ikbal Ali. *Afghanistan of the Afghans*. London: Diamond Press, 1928.

Spain, James W. *The Pathan Borderland.* The Hague: Mouton, 1963.

Wilber, Donald N. "The Structure of Islam in Afghanistan," *Middle East Journal,* 6, no. 1 (1952), 41–48.

Chapter 2. Historical Setting:
The Struggle for Unity and Independence

As previously noted, the literature on Afghan history is relatively abundant. No one authority had a predominant influence upon the discussion of the pre-Durrani period. For the roles of the Afghan monarchy and British interference upon the building of the Afghan state, Fraser-Tytler (1967), Vartan Gregorian (*The Emergence of Modern Afghanistan: Politics of Reform and Modernization, 1880–1946* [Palo Alto: Stanford University Press, 1969]), Arnold Fletcher (*Afghanistan: Highway of Conquest* [Ithaca: Cornell University Press, 1965]), and Ademac (1967) were of special value. Poullada (1969) was helpful on the Amanullah period as was Gregorian whose detailed history also provided much of the material on the Musahiban period prior to 1947. Also useful for the 1930's and 1940's were Huffman (1951), Sykes ("Afghanistan: The Present Position," 1940), Maillart (1940), Wilber (1952), and Prince Peter of Denmark (1947). For the regimes of Shah Mahmud and Prince Daud, Wilber ("Contemporary Society and Politics in Afghanistan," in *Current Problems in Afghanistan* [Princeton: Princeton University Conference, 1961], pp. 15–23), Dupree, AUFS Reports (1959, nos. 1 and 2; 1960, nos. 3–6, 7; 1961, nos. 2–4; 1963, nos. 1 and 7), and Smith et al., U.S. Army *Area Handbook for Afghanistan* (1969) were principally consulted.

GENERAL HISTORIES

Ali, Mohammad. *A Cultural History of Afghanistan.* Lahore: Punjab Educational Press, 1964.

Caroe, Olaf. *The Pathans, 550* B.C.–A.D. *1957.* London: Mac-Millan, 1958.

Klimburg, Max. *Afghanistan: Das Land im Historischen Spannungsfeld Mittelasiens.* Vienna: Oesterreichischer Bundesverlag, 1966.

Masson, Vadim M., and Vadim A. Romodin. *Istoriya Afganistana* (History of Afghanistan). 2 vols. Moscow: Nauka, 1964–1965.

Pazhwak, Abdur Rahman. *Aryana (Ancient Afghanistan).* Hove, England: Key Press (1954?).

Sykes, Sir Percey M. *A History of Afghanistan.* 2 vols. London: MacMillan, 1940.

PROTO-NATIONAL HISTORY

Barthold, Wilhelm. *Turkestan down to the Mongol Invasion.* 2d ed. London: Luzac, 1928.

Bosworth, Clifford E. *The Ghaznavids: Their Empire in Afghanistan and Eastern Iran, 994–1040.* Edinburgh: Edinburgh University Press, 1963.

Tarikh-i-Afghanistan (History of Afghanistan). 3 vols. Kabul: Matba 'eh-yi-umumi, n.d. and 1946. The first volume, by A. A. Kohzad and M. U. Sidqi, concerns the ancient period through Alexander the Great. The second, by A. A. Kohzad, completes the pre-Islamic era and the third, by M. Ghubar and A. A. Na'imi, brings the narrative near the end of the ninth century A.D.

Tarn, W. W. *The Greeks in Bactria and India.* 2d ed. Cambridge: Cambridge University Press, 1951.

HISTORY OF THE AFGHAN NATIONAL STATE TO 1929

Ademac, Ludwig W. *Afghanistan 1900–1921: A Diplomatic History.* Berkeley: University of California Press, 1967.

Davies, C. Collin. *The Problem of the Northwest Frontier, 1890–1908, with a Survey of the Policy since 1849.* Cambridge: Cambridge University Press, 1932.

Dodwell, H. H., ed. *The Cambridge History of the British Empire:* Vol. 4, *British India, 1497–1858.* Cambridge: Cambridge University Press, 1929. Chapter 27, "Afghanistan, Russia, and Persia," by W. A. J. Archbold covers the early nineteenth century.

Fraser-Tytler, Sir William Kerr. *Afghanistan: A Study of Political Developments in Central and Southern Asia.* 3d ed., revised by M. C. Gillett. New York: Oxford University Press, 1967.

Gray, John Alfred. *At the Court of the Amir.* London: MacMillan, 1901. Memoirs of an adviser to Abdur Rahman.

Habberton, William. *Anglo-Russian Relations Concerning Afghanistan, 1837–1907.* Urbana: University of Illinois Press, 1937.

Hanna, Henry B. *The Second Afghan War, 1878–79–80: Its Causes, Its Conduct, and Its Consequences.* 3 vols. Westminster and London: Constable, 1899, 1904, 1910.

Kakar, M. Hasan. "The Consolidation of Central Authority in Afghanistan under Amir 'Abd al-Rahman, 1880–1896." Thesis 20055, School of Oriental and African Studies, University of London, 1968.

Kapur, Harish. *Soviet Russia and Asia, 1917–1927: A Study of Soviet Policy towards Turkey, Iran, and Afghanistan.* Geneva: M. Joseph, 1966.

Kohzad, Ahmad Ali. *In the Highlights of Modern Afghanistan.* Kabul: Government Printing House, n.d. A collection of articles on nineteenth-century Afghanistan based upon documentary sources.

———. *Men and Events through Eighteenth and Nineteenth Century Afghanistan.* Kabul: Government Printing House, n.d.

Kushkaki, Burhan al Din. *Nadir-i-Afghan* (Nadir the Afghan). Kabul: Matba'eh-yi-umumi, 1931. A well-documented biography of Nadir Shah prior to his assumption of the throne in 1929.

Lal, Mohan. *Life of the Amir Dost Mohammed Khan of Kabul, with His Political Proceedings towards the English, Russian, and Persian Governments, Including the Victories and Disasters of the British Army in Afghanistan.* 2 vols. London: Longman, Brown, Green, and Longman, 1846. A detailed account of events leading to the first Anglo-Afghan war and the war itself by an Indian who participated in the negotiations with Dost Mohammed.

Lockhart, Lawrence. *The Fall of the Safavi Dynasty and the Afghan Occupation.* Cambridge: Cambridge University Press, 1958. An account of the Ghilzai conquest of Iran in the 1720's.

Macrory, Patrick A. *Signal Catastrophe: The Story of the Disastrous Retreat from Kabul, 1842.* London: Hodder and Stroghton, 1966. Published in the United States as *The Fierce Pawns.* Philadelphia: J. P. Lippincott, 1966.

Martin, Frank A. *Under the Absolute Amir.* London and New York: Harper and Brothers, 1907. An engineer's account of his experiences while serving Abdur Rahman and Habibullah.

Melia, J. *Visages royant d'Orient.* Paris: Bibliotheque Charpentier, 1930. Pages 5–72 provide a description of the reign of Amanullah.

Mir Munshi, Sultan Muhammad Khan. *The Constitution and Laws of Afghanistan.* London: John Murray, 1900. Describes the legal system developed by Abdur Rahman.

——, ed. *The Life of Abdur Rahman, Amir of Afghanistan.* 2 vols. London: John Murray, 1900. Largely autobiographical account of the amir's life, edited by one of his chief officials.

Molesworth, Lieutenant General George N. *Afghanistan, 1919: An Account of Operations in the Third Afghan War.* Bombay: Asia Publishing House, 1962.

Poullada, Leon B. "Political Modernization in Afghanistan: The Amanullah Reforms." In George Grassmuck et al.,

Afghanistan: Some New Approaches. Ann Arbor: Center for Near Eastern and North African Studies, U. of Michigan, 1969. Pp. 99–148.

Rastogi, Ram S. *Indo-Afghan Relations, 1880–1900.* Lucknow: Nav-Jyoti Press, 1965.

Reisner, Igor Mihailovich. *Razvitie feodalizma i abrazaovanie gosudarstvau Afgantsev* (Development of Feudalism and Formation of the Afghan State). Moscow: Izdatel 'stvo Akademii Nauk SSSR, 1954. A Marxist interpretation of the consolidation of the Afghan state since the early eighteenth century.

Rishtya, Sayyid Qasim. *Afghanistan dar garn-i-nuzdahum* (Afghanistan in the Nineteenth Century). Kabul: Matba'eh-yi-umumi, 1950.

Schwager, Joseph. *Die Entwicklung Afghanistans als Staat und seine zwischenstaatlichen Beziehunger.* Leipzig: Noske, 1932.

The Second Afghan War, 1878–1880: Official Account. Intelligence Branch, Army Headquarters, India. London: John Murray, 1908.

Shah, Sirdar Ikbal Ali. "Bolshevism in Central Asia," *Edinburgh Review,* 234 (1921), 136–146.

———. *Modern Afghanistan.* London: Sampson Low (1939?).

Singh, Ganda. *Ahmad Shah Durrani: Father of Modern Afghanistan.* Bombay: Asia Publishing House, 1959.

Singhal, D. P. *India and Afghanistan, 1876–1907: A Study in Diplomatic Relations.* St. Lucia, Queensland: University of Queensland Press, 1963.

The Third Afghan War, 1919: Official Account. Compiled in the General Staff Branch, Army Headquarters, India. Calcutta: Government of India, Central Publishing Branch, 1926.

Viollis, Andre'e. *Tourmente sur l'Afghanistan.* Paris: Libraire Valois, 1930. Describes Amanullah's downfall and Bacha-i-Sachao's regime.

MUSAHIBAN ERA TO 1963

Binava, 'Adb al-Ra'uf. *Pushtunistan*. Kabul: Matba'eh-yi-umumi, 1330 A.H. (1951). An extensive presentation of the Afghan position on Pushtunistan.

Caroe, Olaf. "The North-West Frontier, Old and New," *Royal Central Asian Journal*, 48, no. 3/4 (1961), 289–298. Discusses the Pushtunistan dispute.

Castagne, Joseph A. "Soviet Imperialism in Afghanistan," *Foreign Affairs*, 13 (1935), 698–703.

Dupree, Louis. "The Durand Line of 1893: A Case Study in Artificial Boundaries and Culture Areas." In *Current Problems in Afghanistan*. Princeton: Princeton University Conference, 1961. Pp. 77–93.

Franck, Dorothea Seelye. "Pakhtunistan: Disputed Disposition of a Tribal Land," *Middle East Journal*, 6, no. 1 (1952), 49–68.

Fraser-Tytler, Sir William Kerr. "The Expulsion of Axis Nationals from Afghanistan." In George Kirk, ed., *The Middle East in the War (Survey of International Affairs 1939–1946)*. 2d ed., Oxford: Oxford University Press, 1953. Pp. 141–146.

Gillett, Sir Michael. "Afghanistan," *Royal Central Asian Journal*, 58, no. 3 (1966), 238–244.

Hauser, Ernest L. "Afghan Listening Post," *Saturday Evening Post*, 216, no. 39 (March 25, 1944), 19ff.

Huffman, Arthur V. "The Administrative and Social Structure of Afghan Life," *Royal Central Asian Journal*, 38 (1951), 41–48.

Maillart, Ella. "Afghanistan's Rebirth," *Royal Central Asian Journal*, 27 (1940), 224–228.

Pazhwak, Abdur Rahman. *Pakhtunistan: The Khyber Pass as the Focus of the New State of Pakhtunistan*. Hove: Key Press (1954?).

Peter of Greece and Denmark, Prince. "Post-War Developments in Afghanistan," *Royal Central Asian Journal,* 34 (1947), 275–286.

Smith, Harvey H., et al. *Area Handbook for Afghanistan.* Department of the Army, Pamphlet No. 550–65. Washington: U.S. Government Printing Office, 1969.

Squire, Sir Giles. "Recent Progress in Afghanistan," *Royal Central Asian Journal,* 37 (1950), 14–18.

Sykes, Sir Percey M. "Afghanistan: The Present Position," *Asiatic Review,* 36 (1940), 279–310.

Wilson, Andrew. "Inside Afghanistan: A Background to Recent Troubles," *Royal Central Asian Journal,* 47 (1960), 286–295.

Chapter 3. Government: Structure and Functions

Availability of empirical and analytical data on most facets of contemporary Afghan government is spotty and generally limited. Constitutional reform has inspired some interest among Afghan and foreign observers, but systematic work on the structure, functions, and sociology of government remain almost untouched. Consequently, the existing literature provides little material on which to base detailed analysis of management practices; the recruitment, assignment, and promotion of personnel; local government operations; the civil and political aspects of the military establishment; or, most frustrating of all, definitive information on the transactions and decisions made at the highest levels of government, i.e., within the cabinet or among the informal group of leaders who closely advise the king.

To a large extent the observations on such questions which are made in the chapter are based upon the author's personal contact with Afghans and others who have been active in administration, politics, or development. Needless to say many of the conclusions drawn are tentative and await correction or amplification with the development of monographic literature. Useful accounts of government can be found in

Vartan Gregorian (*The Emergence of Modern Afghanistan: Politics of Reform and Modernization, 1880–1946* [Palo Alto: Stanford University Press, 1969]), Leon B. Poullada ("Political Modernization in Afghanistan: The Amanullah Reforms," in George Grassmuck et al., *Afghanistan: Some New Approaches* [Ann Arbor: Center for Near Eastern and North African Studies, U. of Michigan, 1969]), Afghanistan Ministry of Education, *Manpower and Education* (1969), H. F. Schurmann (*The Mongols of Afghanistan* [The Hague: Mouton, 1963]), the Kabul *Times Annual* (1967), and the Ministry of Planning, *Survey of Progress* (especially 1970). Government policy and operations are prominently featured in the reporting of the Kabul *Times*. The literature on recent constitutional change is more adequate. Gregorian (1969) and Arthur V. Huffman ("The Administrative and Social Structure of Afghan Life," *Royal Central Asian Journal*, 38 (1951), 41–48) provide sound summaries of the structure and functioning of the 1931 Constitution. The most exhaustive reporting and analysis of the 1964 Constitution have been done by Dupree, AUFS Reports (1965, nos. 1–4, 10).

Ahmad, Mohammad B. "Constitutions of Eastern Countries." In *Select Constitutions of the World*. 2d ed., vol. I. Karachi: Governor General's Press and Publications, 1951.

Constitution of Afghanistan, October 1, 1964. Kabul: Education Press, 1964.

Dupree, Louis. "Afghanistan: The Political Uses of Religion." In K. H. Silvert, ed., *Churches and the State: The Religious Institution and Modernization*. New York: American Universities Field Staff, 1967. Pp. 195–212.

———. "Tribal Traditions and Modern Nationhood: Afghanistan," *Asia*, 1 (1964) 1–12.

———. "Tribalism, Regionalism, and National Oligarchy: Afghanistan." In K. H. Silvert, ed., *Expectant Peoples: Nationalism and Development*. New York: Random House, 1963. Pp. 41–76.

Eberhard, Wolfram. "Afghanistan's Young Elite." In Wolfram Eberhard, *Settlement and Social Change in Asia.* Hong Kong: Hong Kong University Press, 1967. I, 397–414.

Halpern, Manfred. *The Politics of Social Change in the Middle East and North Africa.* Princeton: Princeton University Press, 1963.

Karimi, Ahmadullah Khan. "The Constitution of Afghanistan," *Afghanistan,* 1, no. 1 (1946), 3–8.

Malyshev, Iu I. "Iz istorii konstitutsionnogo razvitiia Afganistana" (From the History of Afghanistan's Constitutional Development). Voprosy gasudarstva i prava. Ama Alta: 1963.

———. "Korol' i pravitel 'stvo v gosudarstvennoi sisteme sovremonnogo Afganistana" (The King and the Government in the Contemporary State System of Afghanistan). UTKVIGMP, 1964.

Wilber, Donald N. "Contemporary Society and Politics in Afghanistan." In *Current Problems in Afghanistan.* Princeton: Princeton University Conference, 1961. Pp. 15–23.

———. "Document: Constitution of Afghanistan," *Middle East Journal,* 19, no. 2 (1965), 215–229.

Chapter 4. The Economy:
Internal Growth and External Aid

Recent changes in the Afghan economy have been documented more completely than other facets of the society. A modest deluge of reports by the Afghan government and by foreign assistance agencies together with books and articles by journalists and scholars have unevenly but materially added to the understanding of the nature of the economy and how it has responded to new stimuli. Perhaps the most marked improvement is the coverage and growing accuracy of economic statistics. In the 1960's, data on such basic economic elements as foreign trade and exchange, internal prices, credit, taxation, industrial and agricultural production, mineral resources, and labor force estimates have become available and reliable enough to use. Important limitations remain. Human and animal censuses and comprehensive land and income surveys await the future.

Nearly all of the recent statistical data provided in the chapter is taken from the most recent *Survey of Progress* published by the Afghan Ministry of Planning. Figures on the earlier phases of foreign trade and foreign aid have come from Franck (1960) and the second and third five-year plans. Educational figures have largely come from the Ministry of Education's 1969 report on *Manpower and Education*. Recent development strategies and the results achieved since 1967 have been based upon materials provided by the *Survey of Progress* (1970); the Kabul *Times;* the *Third Five-Year Plan;* and such U.S. government publications as the Department of State's *Background Notes on Afghanistan, June, 1968,* the U.S. Embassy, Kabul, *Annual Economic Trends Report, June, 1970;* and USAID, Kabul, *Status of All Projects Financed through Foreign Aid for Afghanistan's Development, June, 1970.* Interviews with officials of the Afghan Embassy, Washington, and the U.S. State Department have also proved helpful on recent economic developments. Asterisked items are available through USAID, Washington.

Afghan Embassy, London. *Afghan Progress in the Third Year of the Plan.* London: (1960).
——. *Afghan Progress in the Fifth Year of the Plan.* London: (1961).
* Anderson, Clay. *A Banking and Credit System for the Economic Development of Afghanistan.* Report to the Royal Government of Afghanistan. Washington: Robert Nathan Associates, 1967.
* Benz, John S., and N. Holmgren. *The Helmand Valley: An Overall View.* Report to USAID-Afghanistan, 1962.
* Byroade, H. A. *The Changing Position of Afghanistan in Asia.* Washington: Department of State, 1961.

Cervinka (Cervin), Vladmir. *Afghanistan: Structure économique et sociale: Commerce extérieure.* Lausanne: Office Suisse d'Expansion Commerciale, 1950. Valuable study of conditions during the 1930's and 1940's.

Chernyakovskaya, Neonila Ivanovna. *Razvitiye promyshlennosti i polozheniye rabochego klassa Afganistana* (Development of Industry and Position of the Working Class of Afghanistan). Moscow: Nauka, 1965.

——. "Ekonomisheskie positsee imperialisticheskikh derzhav v sovermennom Afganistane" (The Economic Positions of the Imperialist Powers in Contemporary Afghanistan). Voprosy ekonomiki Afganistana. Moscow: I.V.L., 1963. Pp. 157–195.

Davydov, A. D. *Agrarnyi stroi Afganistana: osnovnye etapy razvitiia* (Main Stages of Development of the Agricultural System in Afghanistan). Moscow: Nauka, 1967.

Ekker, Martin H. *Economic Aspects of Development of Afghanistan.* New York: United Nations, 1952. Valuable appraisal of development prospects in the early 1950's by an adviser furnished by the U.N.

Eltezam, Z. A. "Afghanistan's Foreign Trade," *Middle East Journal,* 20, no. 1 (1966), 95–103.

Franck, Peter G. "Afghanistan: A New Day is Dawning," *Middle East Report,* 7, no. 6 (1954), 3 unnumbered pages.

——. *Afghanistan between East and West.* Washington: National Planning Association, 1960.

——. "Economic Progress in an Encircled Land," *Middle East Journal,* 10, no. 1 (1956), 43–59.

——. "Foreign and Economic Development in Afghanistan." Unpublished Ph.D. Thesis, University of California, Berkeley, 1954.

——. *Obtaining Financial Aid for a Development Plan: The Export-Import Bank of Washington Loan to Afghanistan.* Washington: U.S. Government Printing Office, 1954.

——. "Problems of Economic Development in Afghanistan," *Middle East Journal* 3, no. 3 (1949), 293–314; 421–440.

——. "Technical Assistance through the United Nations: The Mission in Afghanistan." In Howard M. Teaf, Jr., and Peter G. Franck, eds., *Hands across Frontiers*. Ithaca: Cornell University Press, 1955. Pp. 13–61.

Golovin, Iu. M. *Sovetskii Soiuz i Afganistan: Opvt ekonomicheskogo sotrudnichestva* (The Soviet Union and Afghanistan: A Test of Economic Cooperation). Moscow: I.V.L., 1962.

Guha, Almalendu. "Economic Development of Afghanistan, 1929–1961," *International Studies* 6 (1965), 421–431.

* Hinrichs, Harley H. *The Role of Public Finance in Economic Development in Afghanistan*. Report to the Royal Government of Afghanistan. Washington: Robert Nathan Associates, 1967.

Jabcke, Peter. "Economic Development in Afghanistan and Its Obstacles," *Asian Studies* (Manila), 6, no. 2 (1967), 345–357.

Karhaneh (Agriculture). Quarterly publication of the Minisof Agriculture, Government of Afghanistan, since 1952.

Kayoumi, A. H. "La Banque Centrale d' Afghanistan et son Role dans le Developpement du Pays." Ph.D. Dissertation, University of Neuchatel, 1966.

Kukhtin, V. G. "Prolbema tranzita v ekonomike i politikie Afganistana" (The Problem of Transit in the Economics and Politics of Afghanistan). Voprosy ekonomiki Afganistana. Moscow: I.V.L. Pp. 3–56.

"Labour Legislation in Afghanistan," *International Labour Review*, 57 (1948), 83–85.

Michel, Aloys A. "Foreign Trade and Foreign Policy in Afghanistan," *Middle Eastern Affairs*, 12, no. 1 (1961), 7–15.

——. *The Kabul, Kunduz, and Helmand Valleys and the National Economy of Afghanistan*. Washington: National Academy of Science, 1959.

* Moyer, R. T. *An Approach to Economic and Social Development in the Helmand Region*. J. G. White Engineering Corporation, 1965.

Newell, Richard S. "Afghanistan: The Dangers of Cold War Generosity," *Middle East Journal*, 23, no. 2 (1969), 168–175.

* Nyberg, Howard. *An Analysis of Private Investment in Afghanistan*. Chicago: Miner and Associates, 1966.

Paul, Arthur. "The Role of Trade in Afghanistan's Development," *Asia Foundation Program Bulletin*, 29 (1963), 1–5.

* Purdy, Ralph D. *Public School Education in Afghanistan: A Survey of Needs and Proposals for Development*. Report by Public School Survey and Planning Team. Kabul: U.S. International Cooperation Administration, 1959.

Rhein, Eberhard, and A. Ghanie Ghaussy. *Die Wirtchaftliche Entwicklungen Afghanistans, 1880–1965*. Köln/Opladen: C. W. Leske, 1966.

Royal Government of Afghanistan, Ministry of Commerce. *Afghanistan's Foreign Trade, 1335 through 1342 (1956–1964)*. Kabul: Government Printing House, 1965.

———. *Trade Promotion Activities*. Kabul: Government Printing House, 1969.

Royal Government of Afghanistan, Ministry of Education. *Manpower and Education in Afghanistan*. Kabul: 1969.

Royal Government of Afghanistan, Ministry of National Economy. *Afghanistan's Economic Plan and Her Current Difficulties*. Unpublished report, 1949.

Royal Government of Afghanistan, Ministry of Planning. *Survey of Progress*. Published for the following years: 1959, 4 vols. (Kabul: Government Printing House, 1959); 1960 (Kabul: Military Printing Press, 1960); 1961–62 (Kabul: Government Printing House, 1963); 1962–64 (Kabul: Education Press, 1964); 1964–65 (Kabul: Government Printing House, 1965); 1965–66 (Kabul: Government Printing House, 1966); 1968–69 (Kabul: Government Printing House, 1969); and 1969–70 (Kabul: Government Printing House, 1970).

———. *Second Five-Year Plan, 1341–1346 (1962–1967)*. Kabul: Government Printing House, 1963.

———. *Third Five-Year Plan, 1346–1351 (1967–1972)*. Kabul: Government Printing House, 1967.

* Stevens, Ira M., and K. Tarzi. *Economics of Production in the Helmand Valley.* A Report for USAID-Afghanistan, 1965.
* Strauss, A. A. *Industrial Development in Afghanistan: A Forward Look.* Kabul: Robert Nathan Associates, 1965.
USAID-Afghanistan. *Briefing Book: Afghanistan.* Kabul: 1970.
——. *Status of All Projects Financed by Foreign Aid for Afghanistan's Development.* Kabul: 1970.
——. *U.S.A.I.D Program Plan (Afghanistan).* Kabul: 1965.
* U.S. Embassy, Kabul. *Foreign and Domestic Private Investment Law of 1967.* State Airgram, February 1, 1967.
——. *Annual Economic Trends Report, June, 1970.*
U.S. Operations Mission—Afghanistan. *Project Progress Report, June 30, 1961.* Kabul: Program Office, U.S. Operations Mission, 1961.
* Whittlesey, Norman K. *The Marketing System of Afghanistan.* USAID-Afghanistan, 1967.
Yusufzai, M. Baqui. *Gross National Product of Afghanistan, 1337 A.H. (1958).* Kabul: Department of Research and Statistics, Ministry of Planning (1960?).

Chapter 5: Recent Political Development, 1964–1971

Developments which have followed the adoption of the Constitution of 1964 have yet to be subjected to intensive study. Much of the available material is to be found in periodicals and newspapers. Official Afghan press sources, especially *Islah, Anis,* and the Kabul *Times* provide the most detailed coverage of events, but their editorial environment precludes aggressive reporting or incisive criticism of government policies or actions. The private press also deserves systematic study. Its impact beyond the official attempts to muzzle it in 1966 and the value of the light it throws upon the political process have not been appraised.

The materials upon which this chapter is based are consequently uneven in reliability and in several instances they cannot support more than the most tentative conclusions. The most valuable sources include Dupree, AUFS Reports (1965, Nos. 1, 2 and 10; 1966, Nos. 4 and 11; 1968, Nos. 4–8; 1970, Nos. 3–7), Griffiths (1967), and Reardon (1969). Interviews and conversations with Afghan officials and politicians and foreign diplomats and assistance officials in Afghanistan during 1966–1967 and subsequently in the United States have figured largely in the conclusions reached. Personal observation and discussion have provided some insights into the process of Afghan political development, but they are no substitutes for the hard data which scholars must discover for greater understanding than is now possible.

Dvoryankov, N. A. "The Development of Pushtu as the National and Literary Language of Afghanistan," translated in *Central Asian Review*, 14 (1966), 210–220.

Gillett, Sir Michael. "Afghanistan," *Royal Central Asian Journal*, 53, no. 3 (1966), 238–244.

Gochenour, Theodore S. "A New Try for Afghanistan," *Middle East Journal*, 19, no. 1 (1965), 1–19.

Griffiths, John C. *Afghanistan*. New York: Praeger, 1967. An account of the political and economic problems confronting the Maiwandwal cabinet at the end of 1966. Well informed; based largely upon interviews with Afghan officials.

Hangen, Welles. "Afghanistan: Progress toward a Constitutional Monarchy and a Money Economy," *Yale Review*, 56 (1966), 60–75.

Hannah, Norman B. "Afghanistan: A Problem of Timing and Balance," *Asia*, 2 (1964), 18–37.

Pradhan, R. S. "First General Election in Afghanistan," *Foreign Affairs Reports* 15 (1966), 110–113.

——. Growth and Working of Parliamentary Institutions in Afghanistan," *Afro-Asian and World Affairs*, 3 (Winter, 1966), pp. 329–337.

Ramazani, R. K. *The Northern Tier: Afghanistan, Iran, and Turkey*. Princeton: D. Van Nostrand, 1966.

Reardon, Patrick J. "Modernization and Reform: The Contemporary Endeavor." In George Grassmuck et al., *Afghanistan: Some New Approaches*. Ann Arbor: Center for Near Eastern and North African Studies, U. of Michigan, 1969. Pp. 149–203.

Wright, David Glen. *The General Interest Press of Afghanistan: A Survey*. Kabul: 1965.

Suggestions for Further Reading

For the student who wishes to extend his knowledge of Afghanistan, the following English language publications have been selected as the most pertinent.

Ademac, Ludwig W. *Afghanistan, 1900–1921: A Diplomatic History*. Berkeley: University of California Press, 1967.

Caroe, Olaf. *The Pathans, 550 B.C.–A.D. 1957*. London: Mac-Millan, 1958.

Constitution of Afghanistan, October 1, 1964. Kabul: Education Press, 1964.

Dupree, Louis. *American Universities Field Service Reports on Afghanistan*. New York: American Universities Field Staff, 1959–1970.

Fletcher, Arnold. *Afghanistan: Highway of Conquest*. Ithaca: Cornell University Press, 1965.

Franck, Peter G. *Afghanistan between East and West*. Washington: National Planning Association, 1960.

Fraser-Tytler, Sir William Kerr. *Afghanistan: A Study of Political Developments in Central and Southern Asia*. 3rd ed., revised by M. C. Gillett. New York: Oxford University Press, 1967.

Gochenour, Theodore S. "A New Try for Afghanistan," *Middle East Journal*, 19, no. 1 (1965), 1–19.

Grassmuck, George, et al. *Afghanistan: Some New Ap-*

proaches. Ann Arbor: Center for Near Eastern and North African Studies, U. of Michigan, 1969.

Gregorian, Vartan. *The Emergence of Modern Afghanistan: Politics of Reform and Modernization, 1880–1946.* Palo Alto: Stanford University Press, 1969.

Griffiths, John C. *Afghanistan.* New York: Praeger, 1967.

Hangen, Welles. "Afghanistan: Progress toward a Constitutional Monarchy and a Money Economy," *Yale Review,* 56 (1966), 60–75.

Huffman, Arthur V. "The Administrative and Social Structure of Afghan Life," *Royal Central Asian Journal,* 38 (1951), 41–48.

Newell, Richard S. "Afghanistan: The Dangers of Cold War Generosity," *Middle East Journal,* 23, no. 2 (1969), 168–175.

Royal Government of Afghanistan, Ministry of Planning. *Survey of Progress, 1969–1970.* Kabul: Government Printing House, 1970.

Schurmann, H. F. *The Mongols of Afghanistan.* The Hague: Mouton, 1961.

Smith, Harvey H., et al. *Area Handbook for Afghanistan.* Washington: Department of the Army, U.S. Government Printing Office, 1969.

Spain, James W. *The Pathan Borderland.* The Hague: Mouton, 1963.

Sykes, Sir Percey M. *A History of Afghanistan.* 2 vols. London: MacMillan, 1940.

Wilber, Donald N., ed. *Afghanistan.* New Haven: Human Relations Area Files Press, 1962.

——. *Annotated Bibliography of Afghanistan.* New Haven: Human Relations Area Files Press, 1968.

Index

Library of Congress Cataloging in Publication Data
      (For library cataloging purposes only)

Newell, Richard S   , date.
   The politics of Afghanistan.

   (South Asian political systems)
   Bibliography: p.
   1. Afghanistan—Politics and government.
 2. Afghanistan—Economic conditions. I. Title.
 II. Series.
 DS369.4.N44   320.9'581'04   78-176487
 ISBN 0-8014-0688-9